How to Become an Expert Software Engineer
(and Get Any Job You Want)

A Programmer's Guide to the Secret Art of
Free and Open Source Software Development

by Marcus Tomlinson

Publisher: Marcus Tomlinson
Cover & Interior Design: Marcus Tomlinson

First Edition, 2016

DEDICATION

To my wife Lisa, and our son Aaron, without your love and support this book would have never happened!

CONTENTS

ABOUT THE AUTHOR

Marcus Tomlinson is a qualified BSc Software Engineer from Durban, South Africa, with 9 years' experience in embedded and application software development.

Immediately following his university career, Marcus landed his first job at Africa's leading manufacturer of electronic security products: IDS, where at the age of 21, he co-created a revolutionarily new, modular test jig system to help the company keep up with its rapidly growing product demand (A system that is still in effect today).

At 25, he went on to land his first senior development role at the world's largest supplier of military and mining simulators: ThoroughTec, making him the youngest employee to hold the position. During his time there,

Marcus completely and independently overhauled the company's internal audio engine, as well as created a highly successful data-flow framework called: "Circuit Sim", to modularise and simulate complex vehicle control systems.

Since late 2013, Marcus has been working for the open source software giant: Canonical, designing, implementing and maintaining Ubuntu's Unity Shell features and APIs. He currently holds the position of Technical Lead on the Ubuntu Personal team, and has presented at a number of Ubuntu Developer Summits.

PROLOGUE

I'm writing this book to share some real life, practical steps you can take to perfect the art of software engineering and land your dream job. No pie-in-the-sky theories, no fluff, just some simple, straightforward guidelines. I'm a firm believer in practicing what you preach, so the suggestions I make in this book are all things I have personally done to improve my skill set, and as a result, get every job I've wanted.

I've had a relatively short career so far (just over 8 years), and 2 years ago I landed my favourite job yet! Does that mean it'll take you 6 years to land yours? No, not necessarily, but that's a bit of a tricky one. If you're new to the field and the job listing you're interested in states: "6 years' experience required", then perhaps yes, but I truly believe that by following my advice, you'll likely convince them to hire you with fewer years under your belt. Trust me, at 28, I've been the youngest amongst those sharing my title at every company I've worked for. Proving your proficiency in a skill is far more valuable to an employer than simply stating the number of years you've spent doing it.

Ever heard the saying: "practice makes perfect"? There are a lot of bad theories out there, but this is one that I'm sure you'd agree holds a pretty valid point. If you want to perfect anything, you need to practice it, and in the world of software engineering, I see no better way to practice your art than with open source development. Not only is writing open source software a great way to learn and acquire new skills, it is a brilliant way to gain real world experience in something your current job may not be offering you; experience that you can legitimately claim on your résumé. There's no hiding behind the cosy veneer of closed source software here, these are real solutions with real users, but this time your code is as much the product as the application.

So why should you listen to me? Well, if asked to name the world's most successful open source project, most people would immediately answer: Linux. The Ubuntu operating system is arguably the most popular Linux distribution on the planet, and for over 2 years now, this has been my job. Don't get me wrong though, I didn't make a very glamorous entrance to the open source world by any means. I've made a lot of mistakes over the last few years. My personal projects range in popularity from a couple hits a day to a couple hits a month, not to mention one or two utter failures that received zero interest at all! However, it's through these mistakes that I've learnt a lot about the do's and don'ts of free and open source software development, and is precisely why I'm writing this book. I want to show you the system I use to design, develop, and deliver open source software, steer you away from the mistakes I've made along the way, and help you build an impressive résumé of projects that'll get that job you've always wanted!

So, without further ado, let's get started...

PART ONE

Define

CHAPTER ONE

Reprogramming yourself for success

Step 1: Be proud to be an engineer

What ever happened to praising the hard working engineer? The Steve Wozniaks and Linus Torvaldses of the world. We have put managers, directors, and CEO's so high up on a pedestal that many of us actually believe, unless we end up becoming one of these, our career is a failure. We are in the middle of the information age right now, computers are literally transforming the world around us, and we are the men and women shaping it in our hands. Even though the part you play may seem small and insignificant, remember that the whole is far greater than the sum of its parts, your impact on the world is more significant than you might think.

Whether you've just started your career, or you're looking to further it, this book is aimed at anyone with an interest in writing software. Those who genuinely enjoy taking on challenging problems and solving them with an enthusiasm for smart, reliable solutions. As software engineers, we give computers new purpose every day. We bring them to life by imparting pieces of our intelligence to them, we create whole new worlds and ecosystems governed by laws we enforce in our code, but most importantly, we love what we do.

In his book: "Drive: The Surprising Truth About What Motivates Us", Daniel Pink narrows motivation down to 3 key elements: autonomy, mastery, and purpose. Without a genuine interest in what we do, we will never be proud of it, we will never master it, and we will never feel purposed for it. In short, if you are not interested, you are not motivated, and without motivation, you will not succeed.

Although the origin is greatly disputed, it is generally accepted that Confucius was the one to say: "Choose a job you love, and you will never have to work a day in your life". This quote has taken a lot of heat, but I think it's just misinterpreted. The emphasis should be on the words: "have to". If you choose a job you love, you will want to work every day of your life.

Step 2: Prepare to work for what you want

The most valuable asset you could offer a potential employer is experience. Although a qualification can be great for getting a foot in the door, anyone who has worked long enough knows that theory and practice are not often synonymous. Remember, what you are being hired for is to do work, and experience proves that you can do just that (well, it almost does). Years of flying under the radar at a company is hardly going to leave you with many tangible skills. The only valuable form of experience you can gain is the kind you actually worked for, because experience you work for is experience you can demonstrate. Proving your proficiency in the job you're asking for is by far the most convincing argument you can make.

By this point, you've probably gathered that this book is not a get-rich-quick scheme. I'm not going to be teaching you any tricks to cheat the system, or telling you that being lazy is ok. What I want is to help you get your priorities straight and work smarter, but by no means does working smart automatically replace working hard. Hard work spent doing something worthless will always be worthless no matter how hard you work, but hard work spent doing something beneficial becomes more beneficial the harder you work.

A lot of people associate the words: "hard work" with feelings of displeasure. To many of us, the word: "work" is reserved for the stuff we do at our jobs; work we tend to see as benefiting our employer more than it benefits us. When we have this mindset, the harder we work, the greater the gap seems to grow between our employer's benefit and our own. We need to break out of this way of thinking. Sure, hard work is not necessarily fun, but it should always feel worthwhile. If your job does not leave you proud after a hard day's work, you need to find one that does.

Step 3: Take the "dream" out of "dream job"

Earlier, I quoted the maxim: "Choose a job you love, and you will never have to work a day in your life". There are a few variations of this quote out there, the most common being: "If you do what you love, you'll never work a day in your life". Although the intent is still there, in my opinion, this variation has lost the most important element of the original message: The word: "job". You could love the field you're in, but hate the job you have. Unfortunately, many of us are driven into directing frustration towards our field of work, rather than the job that drove us there.

We need to take a step back and remember why we chose this career. Where did we dream of being? What did we dream of doing? Maybe the job you really want is right there in the company you already work for. It could be a shift in the projects you're assigned to, a promotion to higher profile work, or a whole new position entirely. The perfect job could be waiting for you at the company down the road, or across the ocean on a whole other continent. The point is, without aiming high and having a specific job in mind (and actually believing you can achieve it), you'll just continue to spread yourself thin across broad goals that lead you nowhere.

Why do we insist on seeing our dream job as only a dream? Why does it feel so out of reach and intimidating?

Well, my theory is: because all jobs require some level of experience; experience in the work you will only be doing once you actually get the job; experience you almost never have due to a lack of overlap in the work you do at your current job. It's a tricky "chicken and egg" situation, and is why so many of us tend to stagnate on the technologies and domains we started with at our first job. So how do we break from this stagnation? Get back to programming for fun! Your aim should be to eventually land a job doing what you love, and a good indicator of whether you will actually love the job is to see how motivated you are to do it after hours.

Jobs are real, and they exist to be filled. Nobody has ever been turned down for a job because they were perfect for it. The trick is to find a job that will be a perfect fit for you, then get to work on making yourself perfectly fit for it.

Step 4: Put your software where your mouth is

Virtually every job listing you'll ever come across will require one very important document: A résumé. The impression that this document makes on your prospective employer is crucial. Not only does it stand as a representation of you before you are able to represent yourself, it determines whether or not you will get the opportunity to represent yourself at all. Your résumé should already prove that you are perfect for the position you're applying for before you even get the interview. How is that achievable? Well, your résumé should obviously mirror as many of the requirements on the listing as possible, but what will truly differentiate you from the others is having hard evidence that proves you meet them.

There is a famous quote by Linus Torvalds that goes: "Talk is cheap. Show me the code". Simply stating that you possess a skill, or even a good idea, doesn't mean much until you can actually prove it with something tangible. Enter open source software. What better way is there to prove a skill in coding than with code itself? For each new skill you seek to acquire, and for each pre-existing skill you wish to showcase, you should be writing software to demonstrate it, and making the source freely available online. Not only should you make your code clean and readable for the world to see, it should be user-friendly and fully-functional for the world to use. Knowing that your code can be read and critiqued by anyone across the globe is both an excellent source of motivation for you to do your best work, as well as validation to your employer that this is real software with real users.

The title of this step is a play on the words: "Put your money where your mouth is", but there is another reason I've replaced the word: "money" here. In no way am I proposing that you selfishly abuse open source software as a means of making money. In fact, money shouldn't even enter into the motivation you have for your dream job. You should be driven by a passion to do what you love in a job you can be proud of. Trust me, the money will follow, but don't sell yourself short either, you should be paid what you deserve for the position you have earned.

We owe a lot of respect to what free and open source software has done in the world of computing. We should show our appreciation by contributing good free software that is well-written and helpful to ourselves and to others. Good free software that will earn us our dream jobs.

Step 5: Understand what it takes to be an expert

In 1993, a professor at Florida State University by the name of Dr. K. Anders Ericsson published a paper entitled: "The role of deliberate practice in the acquisition of expert performance". The study was conducted with subjects from ultra competitive, high performing fields such as: professional athletes, world class musicians, and chess grand masters, with the aim of determining how many hours of practice it took for them to reach expert level. Dr. Ericsson concluded that it takes around 10,000 hours of deliberate practice to become an expert in almost anything (the equivalent of a full time job for 5 years).

Unfortunately, this "10,000 hour rule" wound up being widely misinterpreted as: "It takes 10,000 hours to become good at anything". I'm sure you've personally experienced when practicing anything that a pretty decent level of proficiency can be achieved in far less than 10,000 hours. So how many hours does it really take to become good at anything? In his book: "The First 20 Hours: How to Learn Anything... Fast!", Josh Kaufman sought out to determine how long it takes for us to learn new skills. Kaufman was particularly interested in calculating the time it takes for us to traverse the steep initial incline of any learning curve from incompetent to proficient, at which point the curve begins to plateau and further advances take longer to achieve. I'm sure you gathered by the book's title that his conclusion was 20 hours. It takes around 20 hours of deliberate practice to learn almost anything and reach a decent level of proficiency, and any time spent practicing beyond that will make you better and better at it.

So what am I trying to say with all of this? Expertise is more often than not measured in the time you've spent practicing. Even then, how can you prove that the time you've put into something was spent deliberately practicing it? Sorry to break it to you but spending 5 years doing busywork at a software company will not make you an expert software engineer. I can't stress enough how valuable it is to possess experience you can actually prove to have earned. Writing free and open source software not only allows you to prove that you have put in the hours, it allows you to showcase the result of your practice in the form of real, working software.

It's time to start investing in your future and getting to

work on building a résumé that'll get you the job you've always wanted, and in time, will earn you the right to call yourself an expert.

Summary

Step 1: Be proud to be an engineer

- As a software engineer, your impact on the world is more significant than you might think.
- This book is aimed at anyone with an interest in writing software.
- Without interest in what you do, you will not have the motivation required to succeed.
- Choose a job you love, and you will want to work every day of your life.

Step 2: Prepare to work for what you want

- The only valuable form of experience is the kind you've worked for and can demonstrate.
- This is not a get-rich-quick scheme, working smart doesn't necessarily replace working hard.
- If your job does not leave you proud after a hard day's work, you need to find one that does.

Step 3: Take the "dream" out of "dream job"

- Many of us direct frustration towards our field of work, rather than the job that drove us there.
- Aim high, reach for your dream job, and believe in yourself.
- Get the work experience you need by programming in your spare time.
- Find a job that will be a perfect fit for you, then work on making yourself perfectly fit for it.

Step 4: Put your software where your mouth is

- Your résumé should contain hard evidence that proves you meet a job's requirements.
- Prove your proficiency in a skill by writing free and open source software to demonstrate it.
- Don't let money enter into the motivation you have for your dream job.
- Show your appreciation to open source by contributing well-written, helpful software.

Step 5: Understand what it takes to be an expert

- Expertise is more often than not measured in the time you've spent deliberately practicing.
- It takes around 20 hours of deliberate practice to

learn almost anything.

- It takes around 10,000 hours of deliberate practice to become an expert in almost anything.

CHAPTER TWO

Choosing which technologies and domains to focus on

Step 1: Visualise yourself in your dream job

We've established that developing free and open source software is an excellent way to learn and practice new skills, but before you get to writing any code, you need to think about what it is you're aiming to practice. Every job will require that you possess a specific set of skills to justify whether or not you will be capable of performing it. These are the skills you should be putting time into practicing, so in order to determine what they are, you'll need to first visualise the job you're aiming for.

Without giving yourself any kind of direction to work towards, you'll end up wasting a lot of time wandering down paths that lead you nowhere. Every piece of code you write to be added to your résumé should be an investment into your future, but what's more important is that you enjoy doing it. Without an interest in what you're writing, you will find it agonising to invest time and energy into it, which you will need a fair amount of in order to achieve anything worth showing off. This is why you should aim for your dream job, not because it's the safe option, or because it'll earn you the most money, but because it will allow you to do what you truly enjoy, and will give you pride in calling it your own.

Imagine now that you're in your dream job. As you visualise it, try to write down as many key characteristics you envision the job to have. What type of company do you work for? Where is the company geographically based? What is your job title? What kind of projects do you work on? Which parts of those projects are you responsible for? How big is the team you're in? Who do you report to? Does anyone report to you? It's ok if you can't answer all of these right now, the aim here is to try and paint a picture of the type of job you're looking for. Even if that picture is still somewhat blurry after this exercise, at least you will have a canvas on which to start filling in the gaps.

Remember, don't be afraid to aim high. The bigger and scarier the goal, the more your heart gets involved in the decision making, and that is exactly where your ambitions should come from.

Step 2: Look for companies that interest you

Now that you have a rough idea of the kind of job you're looking for, it's time to begin smoothing out the edges. Firstly, you'll need to start making some more focused decisions about the problem domain you find most interesting. A problem domain is a more general classification of the work you'll be involved in, devoid of specific tools and technologies like the IDEs, programming languages or frameworks you'll be using. Example problem domains could be: audio/graphics engineering, web development, or game programming, with subdomains such as: low-level audio/graphics engine development, client-side user interface design, and game physics engineering.

A really great way to discover what kinds of domains are

available is to have a look at what the companies around you are doing. Even if you don't end up working for any of them, this exercise can give you a pretty good idea of the types of companies you could work for, and the services they provide. Just as important as finding out what interests you, is finding out what does not. You may have a preconception about your interest in a specific domain, but find by looking at its leading companies, that you wouldn't feel at home in any of them. Perhaps you don't share the views you read in their mission statements, or perhaps the products they make downright bore you. The point is, if enough companies within a particular problem domain don't interest you, it's likely you'll struggle to find one that does.

As far as company directories go, I found LinkedIn.com to be the most complete and user-friendly directory on the web. You can start by typing a few keywords that describe your target domain into the search bar, such as: "web development" or "audio engineering", then filtering the results by "Companies". There are a lot of other useful filter options available such as: company size, industry, and location, but again, the companies you're researching here don't have to be companies you end up working for, nor do they even have to be nearby. The purpose of this exercise is to find the types of companies you're interested in, not necessarily the company itself.

You may need to adjust your search criteria a couple of times in order to nail down the domain that most interests you, but once you do, pick out a few companies that catch your attention, and start reading into what they're all about. Open their LinkedIn profiles, follow their website links, and if you happen to come across any open source companies, browse some of their code. As you encounter any interesting technologies and subdomains mentioned on these pages, add them to the list of job characteristics we began in the previous step. If you see them showing up across multiple companies, mark them with an asterisk to note their particular importance. It's also worth taking the time now to update and filter out any items on the list that you may clarify or change your mind about during this process.

Step 3: Look for jobs that interest you

Hopefully by this point you've at least managed to narrow your career path down to a single problem domain. Right now you may still be unsure about which technologies and subdomains to focus on, but that's alright because the aim of this step is to uncover which specialisations are available, then filter them down to the one or two that most interest you. A good place to start is to take a look at what career opportunities exist, then pick out the types of jobs you'd want to do.

Browsing through available jobs within a particular domain is a great way of identifying the smaller pieces that make up that field of work. For example, web development can be broken down into server-side and client-side, which can be further broken down into subdomains such as: database programming, security management, transfer protocol development, performance engineering, and user interface design. You may find listings that combine a few subdomains into one job, and occasionally some that will even incorporate two or more specialisations from different domains altogether. By making yourself aware of all the available options, you can make better-informed decisions about the direction in which to take your career.

Armed with a problem domain in mind, start searching

the web for any job listings available within that field. Don't limit your searches to listings nearby, the aim here is to identify what kind of job you find most appealing rather than the actual position you will be applying for. I can't say that I specifically favour one site over the others here, or that I am aware of any particular sites you should avoid, but some of the most notable job search engines are: CareerBuilder.com, FlexJobs.com, indeed.com, LinkUp.com, Monster.com, SimplyHired.com, and again, LinkedIn.com.

As you scan over the available jobs in your domain, take a look at the list of requirements for each of them. From these requirements, try to focus your attention onto one or two specialisations that regularly mention subdomains and technologies you're most interested in, then add the requirements for those jobs to your list from the previous step. If some of these overlap with characteristics already on the list, or if they appear multiple times across different job listings, mark them with an asterisk. If there are items on the list that no longer apply to the specialisation(s) you're now focusing on, remove them.

Throughout this exercise try to imagine yourself in the

job. Imagine yourself working on the associated problems, with the associated technologies, and think about whether you'd be genuinely interested in it. If you find your enthusiasm beginning to deteriorate the deeper you dive into a particular specialisation, you should consider recalibrating your vision to one that better captures your interests.

Step 4: Define a specific career goal

So far in this chapter, we have been gathering what is essentially the extensive list of requirements you would need to get almost any job within your chosen area of interest. The problem is, there is almost certainly more items on that list than time you have, or are even willing to spend preparing only for your career to get started. We need to filter this list down to a few key characteristics that clearly define the specific career goal you're aiming for. As we will soon see, some of these "requirements" may not even be requirements at all.

During this process, I have been intentionally steering your focus away from seeking out the specific job you'd want to apply for, and encouraging that you instead focus on the types of companies and jobs you find interesting. This is because opportunities come and go, and unfortunately you can not guarantee that an opportunity will still be there when you're ready to take it. However, jobs for a particular specialisation are, for the most part, cut from the same mould. By analysing a few related listings, you should be able to filter down and assemble a common set of traits that define the core requirements needed for any variation of that job. The good news is, you've already done the hardest part of this analysis by assembling your combined list of requirements. It's time now to start filtering it.

Up front, you can be fairly confident that the entries on your list marked with asterisks will be the items you should keep. These are the requirements that appeared multiple times during your research, and are pretty certain to keep appearing on these sorts of listings. Still, it's worth running through them now and filtering out any items that you feel are either too specific to a subdivision of the job you're not interested in, or are already covered by other items on the list.

Now split the rest of the non-asterisked items into

technologies and subdomains. As you run through the list of technologies, decide whether it is really necessary that you focus on learning these specific tools, languages, libraries, etc. or whether it is actually more important that you study the subdomains they belong to. Considering that these technologies showed up only once during your research, it's likely that most of them can be filtered out, and that the subdomains under which they fall are really what you should be focusing on. Of course, any technologies on this list that you are particularly interested in learning, and contribute sufficiently towards demonstrating your understanding of the subdomain, should be kept.

All that is left to do now is to clean up the list of remaining subdomains. Again, try to filter out as many of these as possible. If a subdomain relates to any technologies you still have on the list, you should keep it, but other than that, because these requirements appear so infrequently, they are very unlikely to be important.

Step 5: Get your priorities straight

By now you should have a focused and complete list of

technologies and domains that clearly define the specific career goal you're aiming for, however, we're not quite ready to get our hands dirty just yet. Before you can get started, you will need to figure out where the start is. We need to prioritise this list into some sort of order you can follow from top to bottom.

One of the worst things you can do when taking on a new challenge is to set yourself up for a tedious start. It's far easier to leap over a large obstacle with a bit of momentum, than to attempt it from standing. The order in which you arrange the items on your list should allow you to get started on something relatively familiar, while at the same time optimising the ramp up time required for you to develop a respectable momentum.

For the first iteration over your list, try to rearrange the items in the order of interest you have for them from highest to lowest, then assign each of them an interest level rating out of 10. Having a keen interest in the items you take on first should do wonders for your enthusiasm in getting the process rolling, but they could also set you up for disappointment if they turn out to be less exciting than you expected. This leads us to our next iteration.

For the second iteration, assign each item a rating out of 5 on how much previous experience you've had with it. Here is where familiarity enters into the equation. Add both ratings for each item together, and rearrange the list in order of score from highest to lowest.

Lastly, for each group of items that share the same score, move those that have an asterisk to the top of the group, and those that do not to the bottom. If you have any trouble deciding on which order to arrange multiple asterisked and non-asterisked items, prefer interest over experience.

Don't worry too much about getting your list in perfect order right now, the main objective here is really to determine which items you should begin with. As you work through the list on numerous projects, you may find that a couple of readjustments will be needed along the way. Just remember to enjoy yourself. When in doubt, prioritise tasks that interest you over those that may seem smaller, easier, or more familiar.

Summary

Step 1: Visualise yourself in your dream job
- You should be putting time into practicing the specific set of skills required for your dream job.
- Every piece of code you add to your résumé should be an investment into your future.
- Visualise your dream job and write down as many key characteristics you envision it to have.

Step 2: Look for companies that interest you
- Decide on which problem domain to focus on.
- Use Linkedin.com to find the kinds of companies you're interested in.
- If enough companies within a particular problem domain don't interest you, pick another.
- Add any interesting technologies and subdomains you encounter to your list from Step 1.

Step 3: Look for jobs that interest you
- Decide on which technologies and subdomains to focus on.
- Use job search engines to find the kinds of jobs you're interested in.

49

- If enough jobs within a particular problem domain don't interest you, pick another.
- Add any interesting technologies and subdomains you encounter to your list from Step 2.

Step 4: Define a specific career goal

- Jobs for a particular specialisation are, for the most part, cut from the same mould.
- Mark duplicate entries on your list with an asterisk as these will almost certainly be required.
- Most technologies and subdomains that appear only once can be filtered out.

Step 5: Get your priorities straight

- Assign each item on your list an interest level rating out of 10.
- Add to each item a rating out of 5 on how much previous experience you've had with it.
- Split asterisked and non-asterisked items, then rearrange each set according to total score.
- Recombine the list with asterisked items at the top and non-asterisked items at the bottom.

PART TWO

Design

CHAPTER THREE

Coming up with a good project idea

Step 1: Pick a concentrated subject matter

When I first got into writing open source software, I spent a lot of time trying desperately to convince my friends to get into it as well, but the most common response I got was: "I wouldn't know what to write about". Although I can understand that coming up with a good project idea is fairly tricky, I was not all that convinced that this was the only hurdle my friends worried about. When faced with the idea of putting our names onto something so widely available, we naturally get a little anxious. You could have the most amazing project idea ever imagined, but if you allow yourself to be crippled by the fear of rejection, it will never see the light of day. In order to get over this fear, we need to first understand what causes projects to fail, then plan to avoid those mistakes up front.

Projects fail when they do not deliver on what they promise. It's rare, if not unheard of, for an application or library to be considered a failure because it serves only one purpose. A project that promises only to do one thing, then does that thing well, is far more valuable than one that promises many features and delivers on only a few of them. In fact, even those successful in delivering many features run the risk of being overlooked if they are considered too complicated to use, or are perceived to be unstable due to high maintenance costs. Rather do simple well, than complex badly. People will hardly have much to complain about if you're honest with your claims, and deliver on them accordingly. Besides, let's not forget that you're giving your software away for free, from my experience, the audience can be pretty forgiving.

With all of this in mind, have another look at your list of technologies and domains from the previous chapter. If it is possible, take only the top item from that list and try to concentrate on showcasing just this particular skill in your next project. If you feel strongly that the next item on the list would pair well with the first, feel free to take on both at once, but do try to avoid muddying up the intension of your project with functionality that is only loosely related. Your aim should be to focus on a concentrated subject matter that will allow you to showcase your particular understanding of the topic, and will result in a clean and simple product with a clear purpose. A good example of two items that pair well together is a programming language and a subdomain.

Step 2: Look for problems that need solving

The next fork in the road we must overcome towards coming up with a good project idea is to determine exactly what problem(s) our software aims to solve. It was by no mistake that software marketers began labelling our products as "software solutions". The name clearly implies that software is created to solve problems, but many people seem to disagree with this correlation. I feel that it really comes down to your definition of the word: "problem". A problem is more readily associated with a complication or a source of difficulty, but it can also simply refer to an unresolved query, an anticipated need, or an intriguing challenge. In my opinion, either definition can be used to describe software, and hence, both can be leveraged as inspiration for good project ideas.

Right now, you may not yet be sure whether your project should be a full-blown application, or whether it should be a library of useful functionality utilised by other applications. Either way, you're almost certainly going to be incorporating libraries into your project. It is good practice, when developing any application, that you define a clear abstraction between your back-end and front-end code. Your back-end should consist of a library, or collection of libraries that serve up an API to the front-end, and your front-end should do little else than to consume that API and implement user interface logic. Remember, the entire composition of your project should stand to impress your future employers. A piece of furniture built with rotten wood is destined to crumble under pressure, no matter how beautiful the veneer is. Therefore, regardless of whether you're writing an application or a library, at least some of your time will be spent developing its API. An API that programmers, like yourself, can use to create applications.

Considering now that developers are at least our initial

audience, let's do some research into what kind of problems exist for them. The best website for developer Q&A has got to be StackOverflow.com. Browse to StackOverflow.com and switch to the "Tags" view. Tags categorise questions into groups of related issues, and therefore are very helpful in finding problems specific to a certain technology or domain. You can start by typing a few keywords that describe the topic of your project into the search bar, then selecting the tag that best suits your subject matter. You can further refine the search by adding more tags, or by typing additional keywords into the search bar.

Once you have filtered the results down to a series of questions directly related to your subject matter, start scanning through them and note down any common issues or themes that appear. Many people with the same problem is a good indication that a decent library or application for it is needed, or perhaps missing entirely. If your subject matter is a technology, finding questions that are directly related to it should be relatively painless, but if it is a subdomain, try to identify common technologies recommended in the answers, and note these down as well. Don't worry if these notes are a little disjointed at the moment, we will come back to organise them later.

Step 3: Look for gaps that need filling

You should have just enough pieces of the puzzle now to start forming a rough outline of your project. You have selected your subject matter, collected notes on a few potential features, now it's time to piece together some more distinctive characteristics. In almost any area of expertise, learning from the failures and successes of those who came before you is an excellent source of inspiration, and the wonderful thing about open source software is that we have direct access to the recorded history of their experiences. The amount of open source projects currently available online is colossal, but as you will soon see, this is more a blessing than it is a curse.

When adding a new project to an already very large global repository, it can easily go unnoticed. The reason for this is usually that the subject matter chosen already has a fairly saturated market, and therefore can quickly blend into the background. That said, your aim should be to bring something new to the table, but before you can determine what new will be, you must first establish what current is, and old was. This is where having a treasury of open source projects really comes in handy. Having a look at what existing projects do and don't do is both a rich source of inspiration for ideas, and a great way of identifying new angles that your project can take to stand out from them.

My default for finding open source software is SourceForge.net. There are a number of alternatives out there, but I find that most, if not all of them intentionally limit their selection to a set of fixed requirements such as: specific version control systems, acceptable licenses, binaries only, limited storage space, and strict access control. SourceForge.net's database is massive, yet easy to navigate, and offers support for both binary downloads as well as various version control tools. What really wins it for me however, is the wealth of detailed statistics they have for every project.

Open up SourceForge.net and start searching for terms that describe your subject matter, as well as any specific functions your project may aim to provide from the research you did in the previous step. Sort the results by popularity, then take a look at the top 5 items that best suit your criteria. For each project, read through the reviews and note down any aspects that people particularly like or dislike about it. Secondly, either download a copy or browse the source online, and try to gauge what can and can't be done with it, then note this down as well.

As you learn about these projects, ask yourself how your approach can stand out from theirs. What features are they missing? Are the technologies they use old and outdated? Do their developers still maintain them? Are they too complex? Could they do with better abstraction, or are they simply trying to do too much?

This process will probably uncover a horde of projects that all do the same thing you want to do, but try not to get overwhelmed by it. This is actually a good sign that this kind of solution is in high demand. Besides, many of them are likely to be poorly executed anyway.

Step 4: Decide whether to create or contribute

As you get closer to settling on a good concept for your project, you may start to wonder whether creating a whole new solution is really the best direction to take, or whether contributing to an already existing one would be the smarter choice. While both are noble in their own right, it is important that you keep in mind that every bit of code you add to your résumé should be an investment into your future. So before you jump into taking on either of them, you should establish which of the two will be the better investment of your time. Let's begin by weighing up the advantages and disadvantages of each approach.

There are a lot of really great advantages to be gained by creating a new project. Taking responsibility for the entire development of a product from start to finish shows that you are flexible enough to be slotted into any phase of the development cycle. Creating something from nothing also displays a keen ability to take initiative and be creative when faced with a problem. Possibly the greatest advantage however, is the educational benefit of having to learn a subject intimately in order to produce a solution for it. Of course, there can also be disadvantages to this approach. You run the risk of appearing unimaginative by writing something redundant, or perhaps introverted by working alone, but realistically these can be avoided by having a little creativity, and eventually by introducing the involvement of others into your project.

Although I generally lean towards creating, there are definitely advantages to contributing as well. Probably the most convincing argument for contributing to a project is if the act itself is closely related to the job you're aiming to get. For example, if the reliability of a certain open source project directly or indirectly affects the success of a company you aim to work for, aiding in the development of it could earn you significant favour with them. If the company itself is an open source establishment, working directly on their own projects can be a good way to prove your proficiency in their domain before you apply. Another obvious advantage to contributing is that you will be able to showcase your teamwork and collaboration skills. This however, can be a double-edged sword. Even though patching code can sometimes be more difficult than writing it from scratch, relying on the existing work of others could imply that you need to be carried by them.

When deciding on which direction to take, try not to be swayed by a fear of incompetency. You don't have to be an expert in the topic you're writing about in order to produce good software for it. In fact, being an expert can often be to your detriment. I've witnessed many accounts where developers have made poor assumptions about the prior knowledge of their audience, and ended up creating products that were too complex for the average person to use. All you need in your arsenal to write good software is a personal interest in seeing the problem solved. Believe me, "showing off" by writing code only you can understand is more embarrassing than it is impressive. Software is most impressive when it takes something that is usually elite or complex, and makes it easy and accessible to anyone.

Step 5: Establish a clear objective

At this point, you may have a whole bunch of good ideas for your project, but still be a little unsure as to how they all piece together. Focus has been a predominant theme throughout this book thus far, and is exactly the approach we should apply here, but this is easier said than done. Just as important as knowing what to do, is knowing what not to do. Steve Jobs once said: "People think focus means saying yes to the thing you've got to focus on. But that's not what it means at all. It means saying no to the hundred other good ideas that there are. You have to pick carefully. I'm actually as proud of the things we haven't done as the things I have done".

Before we can identify the finer details of our project, we must first visualise the big picture. This step requires a fair bit of intuition. Gather all of your notes from this chapter onto a single page, and take some time now to scan over them collectively. Try to identify any sort of common themes or directions they may be suggesting. It could be that many of the difficulties developers are experiencing lead to one core problem, or perhaps people are simply unaware of any alternative methods to what is currently accepted. As you pick up on these themes, start brainstorming a few simple, one-liner descriptions of the possible libraries or applications you could write. Don't let yourself be discouraged if you find that some notes don't fit into any of your descriptions, it is precisely the aim of this exercise to filter these out.

Once you have collected a few high-level concepts for your project, this is where saying no can get tough. You should really try to centre your attention onto one project at a time, right up until it's release. This way, your mind can fully focus on the immediate task at hand, allowing you to work most effectively by channeling your thoughts towards one clear objective, while at and away from your desk. Another recurring theme throughout this book has been the importance of interest in anything you do. Interest is the great motivator, and motivation is crucial when finding time after hours to work on your project. With this in mind, from the few ideas you now have, pick the one that interests you the most. Don't worry about the level of complexity or familiarity of your options at this point, simply pick the one that you think you'd have the most fun with, and go with it.

Congratulations! You are now ready to start designing and developing your open source project. Don't throw away your notes from this chapter just yet. Once you have taken your project through to release, you may want to come back to these for your next one.

Summary

Step 1: Pick a concentrated subject matter

- Projects fail when they do not deliver on what they promise.
- Rather do simple well, than complex badly.

- Try to concentrate on showcasing just the top item on your list from the previous chapter.

Step 2: Look for problems that need solving

- Software is created to solve problems, hence problems are a great source of inspiration.
- Regardless of what you're making, at least some of your time will be spent developing its API.
- Use StackOverflow.com to find common issues associated with your subject matter.

Step 3: Look for gaps that need filling

- Learning from those who came before you is another great source of inspiration.
- Your aim should be to bring something new to the table.
- Use SourceForge.net to find popular projects associated with your subject matter.
- Note down any aspects that people particularly like or dislike about them from the reviews.

Step 4: Decide whether to create or contribute

- A major advantage to creating is the educational benefit of developing a solution end-to-end.

- A major advantage to contributing is that it can add value to the company you're applying to.
- I lean towards creating as its advantages are greater, and its disadvantages can be avoided.
- All you need to create good software is a personal interest in seeing the problem solved.

Step 5: Establish a clear objective

- Gather your notes from this chapter and identify common themes or directions.
- Come up with some one-liner descriptions of a few project ideas from the above themes.
- Pick the one that you feel you'd have the most fun with, and ignore the rest for now.

CHAPTER FOUR
Designing your product

Step 1: Come up with a good name

You have successfully conquered the first major obstacle towards designing a great product: figuring out what it will actually do. Reaching this point is far from insignificant, you have already faced a number of daunting highway intersections along the way, and have now managed to narrow your options down to a single off-ramp. Although we know that this off-ramp is bound to lead us through a metropolis of valuable experience, we still have a few decisions to make as to which route we take through it. The first decision we must make is what our project will be called.

Giving your project a name may seem like a trivial, non-task, but it is far more significant than you might think. Your project's title should serve two main purposes: it should convey some idea of what the project does, and it should be easy to remember. Even before these purposes are realised however, giving your project a name marks a pivotal point in the design process where concept transitions to reality. It is far more motivating and satisfying to work on something that feels real, than to invest in something still seemingly imaginary.

Let's face it, people can't help but judge a book by its cover, and your project's "cover" is often nothing more than just a name and logo amongst others in a list of search results. That considered, the best way to approach this task is to search for software that does what yours will do, then imagine your project amongst the results.

Browse to SourceForge.net and type a few keywords into the search bar that you would naturally enter to find your own project. Now take a look at the list of results and give some thought to how your project could stand out from them. Identify titles in this list that catch your attention, and consider whether yours could borrow any of their naming conventions. I find that the most distinctive titles are those that directly incorporate the project's primary function. Combining one or two associated keywords into your name has two obvious benefits: it states the project's main objective, and increases its visibility in searches.

Of course the cherry on the top of a good project's packaging is a striking cover image. On most hosting sites, this is just an icon-sized logo that is displayed side-by-side with your project's title. Art is not usually a programmer's strong suit, but ironically it is often the overly complex logos that appear the most unprofessional. Again, have a look at what other successful projects are doing, and try to put together a cover image that is simple, and will subtly convey a sense of professionalism.

Step 2: Write up a project summary

In the previous chapter, you formulated your project's chief objective, now it's time to put it into writing. The aim of this step is to come up with a brief, yet descriptive summary of your software that will eventually appear as the subtitle to your project name. This subtitle is the first, if not the only bit of text people will read when stumbling across your project, so it is vital that by reading it, anyone can immediately tell what your software does.

Your project summary should aim to fulfil a number of important purposes such as: describing its primary function, differentiating itself from others, maximising search discoverability, and doing essentially 99% of the product marketing. Coming up with one or two sentences that can fulfil all of the above is not easy, but it is also not impossible. The most difficult of these goals is search discoverability. If we can achieve this, the others should slot into place relatively easily.

To maximise your project's visibility, your text should contain keywords that people often search for, and there is an excellent online tool for determining just that: Google Adwords. Browse to Adwords.Google.com and create a free account. Start a new "ad campaign" setup wizard and skip to the page that contains the "Keywords" section. In the search bar below this tool, type a few comma separated words and phrases related to your project, then click "Add". Once you've added a few keywords to the list, you will be able to see how frequently they are searched for under the "Search popularity" column. You can also click the "More like this" button next to each result to get more suggestions. Try to stick with keywords that get at least 1,000 searches a month. Inserting these keywords into your project summary automatically fulfils two of the purposes we touched on earlier: describing its primary function, and maximising search discoverability.

Conveying an idea of what your project does is only half the battle though, the other half is marketing. At the core of any marketable product is a convincing sales pitch, or in our case, an elevator pitch. The term "elevator pitch" originates from the idea of having to impress a senior executive during a brief ride in an elevator. Here is where it gets a little tricky, and hence where you will likely differentiate yourself from the others. Finding that sweet spot between being both brief and detailed at the same time is challenging, but I assure you, achieving it will contribute richly towards the eventual success of your project. As an open source software developer, you are only perceived to be as successful as your software is.

Step 3: Create a product wish list

While seeking inspiration for a good project idea, you

collected a set of problems and gaps observed amongst projects within your subject matter. You eventually categorised these under a number of different project objectives, then chose the one that most interested you. The observations that ended up under your current project are all excellent ideas for features, and are precisely the items you should add to your product wish list.

A product wish list is essentially the to-do list of your project, but it is a very particular kind of to-do list. The word: "product" is used specifically to imply that these tasks should contribute towards the end product, but the word: "wish" indicates that not all items need to be fulfilled in order for the product to be useful. The aim of this list is to keep track of the high-level features that your end-users wish to see in your software. For example: "Provide a live chat window to talk with other users" is something you could expect to see on a product wish list, but: "Use WebSocket protocol for live chat back-end" is not.

Gather your notes from chapter 3, and start forming a set of wish list items. Imagine yourself as the end-user of your software and think about which high-level features you would like to see, then write each item down as if you were requesting it from the developer. Avoid requirements that are either too broad or too vague. Try to keep your wish list items short and focused, each clearly defining a single end-to-end feature such that, once implemented, it is immediately usable and the product remains functional and release-worthy.

Don't concern yourself with details on how these features will be implemented behind the scenes, all we care about right now is defining our project's end-user experience. In the end, we are aiming to provide a real working product to our users, regardless of how each of these features are broken down and implemented, this list should be our number one priority through all stages of the development.

Once you have assembled your product wish list, it's worth taking some time now to also assemble your product "not" list. This is a list of all the features your end-users may come to expect from your product, but really do not fall within the scope of what you have envisioned for it. Determining this list up front clearly defines your product boundaries, and helps prevent any future scope creep.

Creating these lists, and eventually making them available online, is both a good way for us to stay focused on our primary objective, as well as to let others know exactly what our product will and will not do.

Step 4: Add research to your design

Behind every innovative software company is an R&D department. This department is staffed by engineers and tasked with developing new products, and is exactly where you and I belong. Although both research and development are equally important in R&D, some of us tend to under appreciate the research portion, while others can severely over emphasise it. Regardless of how much a company may be willing to invest into research, it absolutely must make money to survive. Software companies are very rarely in the business of selling good ideas, as the name implies, they typically make their money by producing software. Therefore, what we should aim for is just enough focused research that will enable us to create smart, simple solutions, no more, no less.

There is a reason why R&D is not called: "D&R". Before you are able to develop a solution to any one of your product wish list items, it is essential that you first fully understand the problem. You have to grasp the "what" completely before you can determine the "how" and "why". Without knowing exactly what it is you're trying to solve, you can not possibly understand how to solve it, nor be able to justify why your chosen solution was the best approach. The other great advantage to research is that it can help steer you away from the clichés, and result in solutions that are more smart than obvious. At the same time, you should avoid doing too much research as this can lead to solutions that are more complex than simple.

I am bringing this up now because I want to emphasise that research comes before development, and therefore should be considered as early as the design phase of your project. Exactly what to research and how much of it will be needed can be determined as you tackle each problem, but the aim of this step is to determine which wish list items require more research than others, then plan to include that research as part of the development.

Assign each item in your product wish list a rating out of 5 on how much previous experience you've had with these types of problems. For example, a rating of 5 indicates that you have solved this exact problem before and can almost entirely copy and paste the solution, whereas 4 could imply that although you have solved it before, it was written in a different language, or was based on a technology you will not be reusing. Now invert the ratings by subtracting 5 from each and removing all negative signs. What you should be left with is a research requirement rating from 0 to 5 per item. We will flesh out the details of these research tasks later in the development phase, but for now we at least have a rough idea of how much research will be needed to solve each problem relative to one another.

Step 5: Plan a viable release schedule

There are four major forces at play in the development of any software solution: budget, time, quality, and scope. While all four limits are typically expected to be fixed, often the reality is that eventually one of them has to give for the others to be met. When developing free software, think of the budget as your energy. Instead of the traditional time and money expenses, you're spending time and energy on your project. Time and budget are usually directly related to each other, and are fixed. In our case, if our development drags on for too long without results, our enthusiasm for it will eventually run dry. Clearly we do not want to compromise quality, so we're left with only one variable force: scope.

In chapter 3, I pointed out that projects fail when they do not deliver on what they promise, and that it is better to do simple well, than complex badly. The same theory applies here. Adjusting the scope of your product between releases allows you to deliver quality pieces of software that are on time, and on budget. Again, as I pointed out earlier, people will hardly have much to complain about if you're honest with your claims, and deliver on them accordingly.

If quality is fixed at maximum, and budget is linked to time, what is a good time limit to set ourselves? Well, the answer to that question is the answer every client wants to hear: as soon as possible. Instead of seeing a deadline as a point in time where all features must be completed, we should look at it as the time period in which we have to get as many features done as possible. By first releasing a functional product with the absolute minimum requirements implemented, your software can be ready for testing and feedback at a very early stage, and can serve as a solid foundation for every new feature you add. Unlike other fields of engineering, we have the convenience of being able to release product updates to every one of our clients with the simple click of a button. We should appreciate how powerful this benefit is, and use it to our advantage.

Taking all of the above into account, have another look at your product wish list, and try identify which item(s) absolutely must be implemented for your project to be usable. Don't sweat the small stuff here, you should aim for just one or two baseline features that will take your product from nothing to something. Now start rearranging the list in order of priority from top to bottom. The top being your minimum requirements, followed by items of decreasing importance as you approach the bottom. If you have trouble deciding the order of some equally important features, I suggest arranging them in the order of how much research will be required from lowest to highest. This will allow you to build up some momentum on the more familiar tasks before hitting the more difficult ones.

That's it, your release schedule is ready. As you complete each item on your product wish list from top to bottom, you should be able to release a new, fully-functional version of your software. Incrementally releasing your hard work is an excellent way to keep your enthusiasm up, as well as to allow you the opportunity to move on to another project when you feel you've learnt enough.

Summary

Step 1: Come up with a good name

- It's more motivating to work on something that feels real, than to invest in the imaginary.

- Your project's title should convey an idea of what it does, and should be easy to remember.

- Use SourceForge.net to find similar projects, then brainstorm how yours could stand out.

- Put together a cover image that is simple, and will subtly convey a sense of professionalism.

Step 2: Write up a project summary

- Your product summary should be descriptive, unique, discoverable, and marketable.
- Use Adwords.Google.com to identify popular keywords for use in your summary.
- Formulate an elevator pitch for your project that is both brief and detailed at the same time.

Step 3: Create a product wish list

- Use the problems and gaps that wound up under your project idea to form a product wish list.
- Write each high-level feature as if you were an end-user requesting it from the developer.
- Also assemble a "not" list containing features that do not fall within the scope of the project.

Step 4: Add research to your design

- You should aim for just enough research to enable you to create smart, simple solutions.
- You have to grasp the "what" completely before you can determine the "how" and "why".
- Assign each item in your product wish list a research requirement rating out of 5.

Step 5: **Plan a viable release schedule**

- The only variable force in software development is scope.

- Adjusting scope between releases allows you to deliver software on time, and on budget.

- A deadline is really the time in which you have to get as many features done as possible.

- Arrange your wish list in order of importance from highest to lowest.

- As you complete each feature, you should be able to release a new, fully-functional version.

CHAPTER FIVE

Setting up an open source project

Step 1: Pick an open source license

I wish that I could tell you that free software is a beautifully simple concept that gives you the liberty to take as much as you want, and do with it as you please, but the unfortunate reality is that the word: "free" means very different things to different people. There is a popular saying in the open source community that goes: "It's free as in freedom. Think free speech, not free beer". Let's face it, most of us want both. When I first started developing free software I was disappointed to find just how many strings were attached to the seemingly "free beer" some projects were handing out. The root of my frustration stemmed from the strict distribution and compatibility limitations these projects were enforcing, via licenses I could not understand. The good news is however, once you do grasp the basics, you can quickly differentiate the projects that are "free" as in "free beer", from those that are "free" as in "free timeshare".

Understanding open source licenses is useful for two main reasons: It enables you to make the right choice of license for your own work, and it allows you to identify if and how third party software can be legally integrated into yours. Up front I'd like to point out that I'm not a lawyer, and this is not legal advice. My aim is simply to provide a very brief overview to my understanding of a few popular licenses, in the hope that it will be helpful. For more detailed information on these licenses and their variations, check out: OpenSource.org/licenses.

Without exaggeration, there are over a hundred open source licenses currently floating around the free software world, but fortunately, they all essentially say the same things. The trick is to identify their subtle differences. Right now, the four most popular licenses being used, covering most of the common copyright enforcement variations, are: Apache, BSD, GPL, and MIT. The differences between these licenses narrow down to four core topics: credit to the original author, protection of trademark, compatibility with other licenses, and protection against patent law.

When integrating third party software into your own, credit to the original author is honoured by simply complying with the associated terms and conditions stipulated in their licenses. This section of the license will typically ask that a specific credit notice be made adequately visible to your users, and may also be accompanied by a few suggestions for its placement and presentation. A protection of trademark clause on the other hand, will stipulate that the original author not be credited in your software at all. Although seemingly opposite, both conditions enforce a similar intent: that the original software's reputation should not be associated with that of its derived work.

Things get a little more tricky when it comes to a license's compatibility with others. This topic is split into two types of compatibility: compatibility with free licenses, and compatibility with proprietary licenses. Of the popular licenses mentioned above, Apache, BSD and MIT are all compatible with both free and proprietary software. This means that a company producing closed, proprietary software is allowed to reuse source code licensed under these copyrights in their products. GPL was created not only to keep its software free, but also to force any software using it to inherit the license, and hence, become free as well.

While the standard GPL is not compatible with proprietary software, there is a variation to this license called: "Lesser GPL" (or "LGPL") that is. This was specially created for open source libraries that want to ensure that their code remains free, while not enforcing that its dependants inherit the same attitude. The gist of how this is achieved is by isolating the library as a separate entity, and having the dependant software dynamically link against it at runtime. Unfortunately, the complexities of GPL don't end there. The strict requirements enforced by this license render it incompatible with some free licenses too. For more details on GPL and its compatibility with other licenses, see: GNU.org/licenses.

Another complex topic that can appear in some license texts is: protection against patent law. This protects users from losing any rights granted to them by the license as a consequence of infringing on patents that other contributors may have introduced. This is enforced by requiring that all contributors implicitly grant to all users royalty-free licenses for any patents they may hold that could apply to their code. Furthermore, as part of the license agreement, if the original patent holder initiates any infringement claim against another user, his or her patent license is immediately revoked. This is commonly referred to as an "anti-patent" requirement and is designed specifically to combat, or at least discourage software patents in general. Apache and GPL are examples of this type of license.

In conclusion, to maximise compatibility, and hence popularity, you're better off sticking with the Apache, BSD, and MIT licenses for your projects. While I would generally suggest you stay away from GPL, I occasionally make an exception for LGPL when it makes sense in a library. When it comes to including third party software into your projects, most of their licenses will be variations of these. Just keep an eye out for any subtle differences, particularly in each of the four core topics mentioned above.

Step 2: Pick a version control system

Throughout this book my aim has been to provide some straightforward guidelines to what I feel are good practices in developing open source software, but really, all of the methods I have described so far can be applied to any software you write. When it comes to utilising a version control system, the same attitude applies. You will not be taken seriously by the open source community, nor by your future employers, if your project's source is not managed by version control.

Before you start writing any code, you should first decide on a version control system in which to store it. This way, your project's entire development history can be recorded, from the first line of code to the last. Having a detailed history of your project's development, in the form of snapshots that can be retraced and meticulously compared against each other at any time, is almost mandatory in producing a successful product. Version control systems provide many useful services such as: release management, synchronisation between engineers, maintaining code stability by isolating and independently versioning experimental development, and of course, providing a highly detailed log of when, why, how, and by whom each change was made.

When it comes to choosing a VCS, there are a lot of options available, but practically, there are only a few worth pursuing. In order for your project to attract as much interest as possible, it is really important that you go with a VCS that is popular. Using a popular VCS not only portrays a sense of professionalism, it also allows for more people to be familiar with the process of browsing and retrieving your code, therefore implicitly portraying to both users and developers that you are open to their participation.

A good way to tell which version control systems are the current front runners, is to have a look at what the top open source hosting sites are supporting. You can find a list of these on the Wikipedia article: "Comparison of source code hosting facilities", under the section: "Available version control systems". The top 5 most supported version control systems right now are: Bazaar, CVS, Git, Mercurial, and SVN. Picking any one of the front runners is a good choice, but I would suggest that you go with the one that you are either most familiar with, or find to be the easiest to use. As you would expect, there is a lot of overlap in how these systems work, and the terminology they use, but it is worth taking a bit of time now to briefly look into each one, and try to settle on the VCS whose workflow makes the most sense to you.

Step 3: Pick a canned hosting site

A good open source project webpage should have at least five key elements: high-level documentation, a bug tracker, access to the VCS, downloadable releases, and some channels of communication for users to get support and updates. Unless manually configuring a web page like this happens to be your current objective, I highly recommend that you avoid the headache of doing it yourself by using a canned hosting site. A canned hosting site is a free online service that provides all the tools needed to run a successful software project under one roof. All you need to do is complete a simple online creation wizard, and within minutes you'll have a publicly available, professional project page.

Not only do these sites offer generous quotas of bandwidth

and disk space (including backups of all your data), the services they provide are designed to be fully integrated. For example: you receive a notification that a bug has been reported, you link the bug to a branch, when that branch is merged, the bug is automatically marked as resolved, and all affected parties receive an email detailing when, why, how, and by whom the fix was made. Leave the project hosting software to the professionals. Let their tools do the busywork for you so that you can concentrate on what's more important: your software.

With a particular version control system in mind for your project, picking the canned hosting site that will support it should be relatively easy. Head back to the Wikipedia article: "Comparison of source code hosting facilities", and have a look now at the: "Popularity" section. Currently, the top 5 most popular canned hosting sites (and there supported version control systems) are: Bitbucket.org (Git and Mercurial), Code.Google.com (Git, Mercurial and SVN), GitHub.com (Git), Launchpad.net (Git and Bazaar), and SourceForge.net (CVS, Git, Mercurial and SVN).

Evidently, there is nothing stopping you from creating

multiple pages for your project across more than one of these sites. For example, my choice of VCS at the moment is Bazaar, so naturally I post my projects on Launchpad.net, but as I've pointed out before, I really like the wealth of features and visibility I get from SourceForge.net, so I also post my projects there with a link to the source code on Launchpad.net. Two of the most useful features on SourceForge.net are: the user review system, and the highly detailed download statistics. These will allow your users, and eventually your employers to quickly and easily measure the success of your projects, and hence, gauge how skilled you are at developing good software.

Step 4: Pick a web hosting site

In this step, we will be registering a simple website for your project. Now, before you start wondering whether I've already forgotten my own advice on canned hosting, let me emphasise the significance of the word: "simple" above. The obvious, albeit intentional, limitation to canned hosting is the inability to freely customise your page's content and appearance, forcing all projects to look and feel the same. I'm not suggesting that you spend hours writing software to host other software, in fact, the kind of website I'm talking about should only take a few minutes to set up, and will give your project a substantial boost in professional flair.

Having a dedicated project website is a bold statement to anyone who may doubt the seriousness of your work. It implies to people that some level of care has been invested into your project, and that it was not just quickly thrown together. Now, I'm not suggesting that the implication of professionalism alone can compensate for unprofessional work, I'm merely encouraging that you give your project an outward appearance that will suitably reflect its inward qualities.

First you will need to select a web hosting plan. Currently, there are three really great free web hosting sites available: Neocities.com, Pages.GitHub.com, and Sites.Google.com. If you want your site to appear a little more professional, and you don't mind spending a little money, all three of these providers support custom domain names. When it comes to picking a domain registrar, GoDaddy.com is generally the accepted choice, but I find that prices don't tend to differ much between them, so you can just about take your pick.

Needless to say, a website is of little use without any content, which brings me to the main purpose of this step. There is a class of software development tool called documentation generators. These tools generate documentation for your software from specially formatted comments in the source code. Most, if not all of these tools allow you to output your documentation as HTML, complete with a root index and separate pages for the various building blocks of your software. All you need to do is add some specially formatted comments to your code, run your generation tool of choice, and push the output HTML to your site. The result is a well structured, professional looking project website that is low cost and high gain. For an extensive list of available documentation generators, take a look at the Wikipedia article: "Comparison of documentation generators".

The obvious advantage to writing documentation alongside your source code in this way, is that it too will be stored in VCS and versioned as the code undergoes changes. If you're using Git, Pages.GitHub.com will be of particular interest to you here. Websites are published on

Pages.GitHub.com via the Git repository system, so in your case, your documentation can be linked to your website directly from the project's version control. While this may be an ideal setup, it's not to say that having to manually push your generated website now and then is really that much of an inconvenience.

Step 5: Create and configure your project

Looking back over all the details you've put together for your project thus far, you should have just about everything you need to create and configure it online. By the end of this step, your project page should be up and running publicly for anyone interested in learning about it, but more importantly for now, ready to manage your source code, log development history, and keep track of your bug and wish lists.

It is a popular misconception that a project must first have some code in it before it is worthy of an online presence. The act of creating a project page, whether manually or via canned hosting, should signify that project's inception. I've already expressed the importance of preparing your version control before writing any code, and that working on something that actually exists is more motivating, but what we really stand to gain here is the wealth of development tools a project page can provide us with from day one.

Browse to the canned hosting site you chose in step 3, sign up, and create a new project. Filling in your project's basic information should be really easy at this point. While designing your software, you already established a name, an icon, a summary, even a list of key features and technologies. In this chapter, you established the version control your project will use, the license under which it will be released, and a URL to its own dedicated website. Simply enter these details into the spaces provided, then finish off with a brief description of your project. Remember to make it unambiguously clear that it is free and open source.

Canned hosting sites will typically run you through an initial setup wizard requesting some of the above information about your project, after which you will need to dig a little deeper into your project's settings to configure the rest. The first important feature you should enable is the bug tracker. To your visitors, a publicly visible bug list is another good sign that this project should be taken seriously. The term "bug tracker" is a little misleading though. A bug tracker is not only useful for tracking bugs, it's also handy for keeping tabs on your wish list items. Find and enable the relevant option for the "bug" or "issue" tracker, then begin by adding all of your wish list items to it. Mark each item as "wish list", "feature" or similar, either by adjusting the "importance" or "severity" level of each, or by tagging them with an appropriate label. Now do the same for your "not" list, setting each item's status to "invalid", "won't fix" or similar.

Last but not least, you'll need to set up your project's version control system. This may have already been done for you, if not, you will need to explicitly enable it yourself, typically by initialising a new "trunk" or "master" branch. This will be the root from which all development branches will originate, and to which only release-worthy code should be committed. Look out for keywords like "code" or "version control" in the settings, and register your trunk branch now. Once registered, you should be provided with a URL to which you can start committing your code.

Now that your page has all the basics one would expect from a professional open source project, it's worth spending a little more time scanning over and configuring any other useful features your canned hosting site may provide, such as: forums, mailing lists, wikis, Q&A, etc.

Summary

Step 1: Pick an open source license

- With free software, the definition of "free" depends on the license used.
- Understanding licenses is useful in licensing your own projects, as well as integrating others.
- Credit to the original author is honoured by complying with the appropriate license terms.
- Protection of trademark is honoured in much the same way that credit to the original author is.
- A license may or may not be compatible with other free or proprietary licenses.
- Protection against patent law grants all users free licenses to any patents used legally in the project.
- Stick with the Apache, BSD, MIT, and LGPL (when it makes sense in a library) licenses.

- For more information on these licenses and their variations, see: OpenSource.org/licenses.

Step 2: Pick a version control system

- You will not be taken seriously if your project's source is not managed by version control.
- A detailed project development history is almost mandatory in producing successful software.
- Choose a VCS that is popular to portray a sense of professionalism and familiarity to others.
- See the Wikipedia article: "Comparison of source code hosting facilities" for popular VCS's.

Step 3: Pick a canned hosting site

- Avoid the headache of constructing a complex project website by using canned hosting.
- See the Wikipedia article: "Comparison of source code hosting facilities" for popular hosting sites.
- You could even create multiple pages for your project across more than one hosting site.

Step 4: Pick a web hosting site

- Your project will be taken more seriously if it has its own dedicated website as well.

- Registering a domain name is optional, but you will at least need to register a web hosting plan.
- Use a document generator to create API documentation for your website.
- See the Wikipedia article: "Comparison of documentation generators".
- Writing documentation alongside your code means that it too will be stored in VCS.

Step 5: Create and configure your project

- The act of creating a project page signifies that project's inception.
- Browse to your chosen canned hosting site, sign up, and create a new project.
- Enable the "bug" or "issue" tracker and add your wish list items to it.
- Enable the VCS and initialise a new "trunk" or "master" branch.

PART THREE

Develop

CHAPTER SIX

Managing a part-time work schedule

Step 1: Divide and conquer

As you know, the principle focus of this book so far has been focus itself. We have spent most of our time going through the motions of filtering and prioritising our career options down to a few concentrated goals. The very same process should be applied to the work we do on our projects. As software engineers, the problems we face are naturally complex, if they weren't, there would be little need for us in the first place. By definition, a complex problem is a system of smaller interconnected concerns that combine to form one intricate issue. In order to conquer a complex problem, we must first identify the subproblems it's made up of, then divide the work into smaller, manageable tasks that we can tackle one-by-one.

Refer back to the release schedule you created in chapter 4, take a look at the very first item on the list, and focus your energy on solving just this problem for now. When compiling your product wish list, we intentionally avoided going into any technical detail on how each of them will be accomplished, now it's time to flesh those details out. What you should aim to achieve in this step is a list of some, if not all of the work items that need to be completed in order for your current feature to be fully implemented.

First and foremost, you should set aside time for research. Even if the research requirement rating you've assigned to this feature is 0, it's important to spend at least a few minutes up front refreshing your memory, or catching up on the latest trends. Of course, as your research requirement approaches 5, determining the specific work items needed will become increasingly difficult, but don't panic, this is precisely why research comes first. It's totally acceptable, even expected, for your tasks list to be updated as you work through it. When forming, and reforming this list, the aim is to try be as specific as possible with the information you have at the time, such that with each iteration it becomes clearer and clearer along the way. At the very least, the item you're currently working on should be well defined, you can always reevaluate what's left to do as you learn more about the problem.

When I'm faced with implementing a new feature I know little about, I will typically start with a generic list of tasks such as: "Research a suitable approach to solving the problem", "locally execute any examples I can find online for the chosen approach", "rework the example code into just the functionality I need", "set up a new, minimal project structure" (if this is the first feature of my project), "define an API with declarations for types and functions I'd expect to see from a high-level", "write some release-worthy test code that uses the API to thoroughly exercise the feature", and "reimplement the example code cleanly behind the API in order for my tests to pass".

Step 2: Practice time management

The Father of English literature, Geoffrey Chaucer once said: "Time and tide wait for no man". This is the harsh reality every engineer must face when working under the pressure of a fast-approaching deadline. The irony though, is that sometimes, if not often, it is our own fault that we end up in these situations. Good time management is a fundamental skill that every engineer should possess, whether it's knowing how to work effectively with the time you have, or being able to estimate how much of it you'll need. Unfortunately, this is not an easy skill to master. Predicting how long a task will take to complete is a lot like predicting the future, however, in the words of American psychologist, Albert Ellis: "The best predictor of future behaviour is past behaviour".

Apart from the obvious advantage of practicing time management as part of your open source development, having some form of time schedule for your project pushes you to keep it moving forward. When working on your own personal projects without a manager, or a team depending on you, it can be far too easy to procrastinate. Don't forget, the reason you're writing this software in the first place is to gain experience towards becoming an expert. Without treating every aspect of your project development professionally, you will only be creating poor habits for yourself.

While estimating the time needed to complete a task is tricky, measuring the average rate at which you get work done is somewhat more feasible. Once you are able to determine how much work can be done in a fixed length of time, you can calculate how much time will be needed to do a fixed quantity of work. I'm sure you've experienced first-hand that the amount of code you write is rarely proportional to the amount of time you spend writing it, so how do we quantify work? The answer is: complexity.

Many engineers may share an ability to take on the same problem and solve it, but the difference between them is the time in which each will take to do it. As you would expect, raising the complexity of a problem, increases the time required to solve it, but what's fascinating is how surprisingly proportional they are to one another. In other words, if a particular problem takes you about two hours to solve, a problem of twice the complexity is likely to take you around four.

Calculating your own personal work rate will allow you to more effectively estimate how long a task of particular complexity will take you to complete. In order to determine your work rate, you will first need to assign a complexity rating to each of your work items, then take note of how long you spend solving each one. After completing a few tasks, you should start to see an average complexity-to-time ratio forming.

The complexity rating we apply to each of our tasks is purely relational. The value assigned to one task simply indicates its level of complexity relative to the others. The hard part is determining exactly to which degree one problem is more complex in relation to another. As the perceived difficulty of a task rises, it becomes harder and harder to accurately measure by how much it is more complex than a simpler one. One way to solve this is by using a Fibonacci-inspired sequence of values, namely: 1, 2, 3, 5, and 8.

Refer back to the work items you formulated in the previous step, and assign each of them a complexity rating from the above sequence of values. If you find that an item on your list requires a rating higher than 8, it is a good sign that the work item is too broad, and needs to be broken down further into smaller, more manageable tasks.

Remember, don't overestimate research. It's better to learn just enough to self-correct and dive into practicing, than to procrastinate on books and websites.

Step 3: Avoid distractions

We have acknowledged that without setting ourselves even a flexible time schedule, we are likely to drag the development of our software on for much longer than necessary. However, while procrastinating on a project can drastically delay its release, allowing yourself to be distracted from the task altogether could potentially kill it. Distractions are barriers to practice. For us to effectively avoid these barriers, we must first learn to identify them, remove those that can be spotted up front, then keep an eye out for any that may creep in during development.

We are vulnerable to two major forms of distraction: those in our physical surroundings, and those in our digital environment. Up front, it is important that you eliminate any obvious disturbances by finding a suitably tidy and quiet space to set up your computer and work from. While the space doesn't necessarily have to be your own dedicated office, the more isolated you are from noise and clutter, the better. Apart from the easily discernible physical disturbances we should avoid, we may have to rid ourselves of a few digital distractions as well. There are a number of ways to isolate work from play on your machine, but arguably the most effective is to create a separate user account dedicated to work. This way, you can focus squarely on developing your software, without other applications and websites tempting you from the sidelines.

Unfortunately, even once you've found a decent place to work, and have removed as many distractions as possible, there are still a few stumbling blocks to look out for during development. Possibly the most common cause of digression in writing software is hitting a point where solving one problem uncovers another. The instinctual reaction may be to treat the new issue as an extension of the first and solve both simultaneously, but this just fragments your attention and typically results in either multiple mediocre solutions, or worse, an ever-growing collection unfinished work. As soon as you reach a situation like this in your code, insert a "TODO" comment, add the new work item to your backlog, and continue on with the original task.

Perhaps the second most common source of digression is premature optimisation. Getting sidetracked by optimising code that already works is extremely time-consuming, woefully addictive, and downright unproductive. As Herb Sutter and Andrei Alexandrescu put it in their book: "C++ Coding Standards": "The first rule of optimisation is: Don't do it", "simple is better than complex", and "correct is better than fast". For every work item you do, try to focus exclusively on solving just the immediate problem at hand, be mindful of how long you're spending on it, and postpone any divergent issues to separate tasks for later.

Step 4: Don't rush

It is immensely gratifying to see your hard work turn into something real. As much as the geek in you may love spending days on a few ingenious lines of code, they are of little use to anybody, especially your employers, if they do not contribute towards an actual, working product. It is tangible results that keep us motivated, and our clients invested. Over the last two steps, we've identified ways to avoid unnecessarily delaying our product's release, but it is equally important that we avoid the other extreme as well.

Taking forever to complete a task at work will hardly impress your boss, but rushing it to completion is just as harmful. Oddly enough, these mistakes are not often mutually exclusive. As is frequently the case when nearing a deadline, many developers end up rushing their work to compensate for the procrastinating they did leading up to it. At the same time, we don't need to break our backs with hours upon hours of solid coding. The aim should be to work smart, stick as close to our schedule as possible, and trust ourselves to recognise a healthy break from plain laziness. Let's be honest, more often than not, we know exactly when we are wasting time.

Working a part-time schedule has its own unique difficulties, trust me, I know. I'm not going to bore you with clichés like: "Consistency is key", "do a little something everyday", or "avoid long coding marathons". We have to accept that life can get in the way, and often for good reason. I don't think I need to tell you that neglecting your family and friends is a bad idea. My advice is simply this: put a few hobbies on hold for a while, work whenever you can find the time, and try to avoid taking breaks that are longer than a week, at least until you reach your project's first release. The great thing about splitting a work schedule into small, manageable tasks, is that it allows you to tackle your project piece by piece as you find the time for it.

So, how much time is enough time to write good software? In the opening chapter of this book, we learnt that it takes at least 20 hours of deliberate practice to acquire a new skill. Even if we skip a few days here and there, that's about 45 minutes a day for a month. Research excluded, our practice begins when we start developing actual software. Whether the code we produce ends up in the final product or not, we are gaining experience by means of practicing the technologies and domains our project requires. If it takes a certain number of hours to learn a skill, then clearly more are needed to effectively use it. Consequently, 20 hours is barely enough time to produce a quality product, but every hour spent beyond that becomes increasingly more beneficial to you and your project. As long as your work schedule sufficiently exceeds 20 hours, you can consider yourself skilled enough to produce a product of sufficient standard.

Step 5: Enjoy yourself

Up until now, I have been expressing how important it is that you treat your open source development as professionally as you would your day job, but I want to stress at this point that "professional" does not necessarily have to mean "boring". Designing a detailed project plan, preparing a viable release schedule, and practicing effective time management, are just a few responsibilities that come with the job. Not only do we learn to get used to them, we learn to greatly appreciate the respect they earn us with our clients, the credibility they give us in negotiating deadlines, and as a result, the freedom they offer us to produce quality software.

I think by now I have made it naggingly clear that the driving force behind anything you do should be interest. More than any other reason, interest should be what motivates you to write software. Developing open source projects ought to be fun. It allows us full creative freedom to invent new and exciting products we can be truly proud of. When you genuinely enjoy doing something, it's hard to do it badly. That said, be easy on yourself. Don't worry about writing every piece of code like it's your last. As you gain experience, you will develop an ability to apply design patterns and idioms to your code more naturally, but until then, don't beat yourself up about making mistakes.

If there was just one thing you could do to always ensure a respectable level of quality in your code, it'd be to simply make it as readable as possible. At the very least, this means: using a brief yet descriptive naming convention for types and functions, commenting regularly on what your code is doing, and adhering consistently to one coding style throughout the project. Whether it's you who reads it later, or somebody else, cleanly written code is an absolute godsend when tracing a bug, or refactoring your work. In the long run, readable code that is broken is still far more valuable than illegible code that is functional. Again, above all, just do your best, be easy on yourself, and easy on your code.

Finally, we're ready to start writing some software! We've done just about all we can to prepare ourselves and our project for development, it's high time we started turning ideas into code...

Summary

Step 1: Divide and conquer

- Focus your energy on solving just the top item of your release schedule from chapter 4.
- The problems we face are naturally complex (I.e. can be broken down into smaller tasks).
- First and foremost, you should create a task for research.
- As long as your current task is well-defined, the rest can be reevaluated as you go.
- Start with a generic list of tasks such as: "define API", "write tests", and "implement back-end".

Step 2: Practice time management

- Good time management is a fundamental skill that every engineer should possess.
- It is far too easy to procrastinate without a manager, or a team depending on you.
- In software development, work is quantified in terms of complexity.
- The complexity of a problem is directly proportional to the time required to solve it.
- Calculate your work rate by assigning a

complexity rating of 1, 2, 3, 5, or 8 to each task.

Step 3: Avoid distractions

- While procrastinating can delay your software, distractions can kill it.
- There are two major forms of distraction you should avoid: physical and digital.
- If by solving one problem you uncover another, postpone it to a separate task for later.
- Avoid premature optimisation.

Step 4: Don't rush

- Rushing a task to completion is just as harmful as taking too long to complete it.
- Put your hobbies on hold, work whenever you can, and avoid taking breaks longer than a week.
- Try to plan a work schedule that exceeds 20 hours.

Step 5: Enjoy yourself

- "Professional" development does not necessarily have to mean "boring" development.
- At the very least, just try to make your code as readable as possible.

- Have fun, be easy on yourself, and be easy on your code.

CHAPTER SEVEN
Writing good software

Step 1: Speak your project's language

I'd like to begin this chapter with a bit of a caveat: there are literally hundreds of programming languages to choose from, and there will probably be even more by the time you read this, so unfortunately, it is far beyond the scope of this book for me to extend any useful language-specific advice to you. If your project requires that you program in a language you have little to no experience with, investigating into the associated tools, technologies, design patterns and idioms specific to that language should naturally form part of your research.

I hope it goes without saying that having a reasonable

understanding of the programming language you're using is paramount to writing good software with it, but I would like to emphasise once again that it is better to read just enough about something to start practicing it, than it is to procrastinate on theory. Don't get me wrong though, I'm not saying that reading a lot is a bad thing. For me, reading about programming is often just as interesting as programming itself. I'm just underlining the fact that when it comes to something as pragmatic as software engineering, the theory can not be fully appreciated until it is practiced.

If I could extend just one piece of advice on learning the ins and outs of a new language or technology, I'd recommend that you start with a good book or two on the subject, rather than jumping directly into blogs and tutorials. While there are a lot of really good resources online, books are generally written with more care, they are often peer-reviewed, and typically cover a larger depth and breadth of the subject matter. To find the best book for your needs, I recommend using Amazon.com. Even if you don't end up buying the book from them, their search engine and review system is incredibly useful in narrowing your options down to the most relevant and top-rated books available. Although there is usually a good reason for books to cost as much as they do, it's not to say that there is a lack of good free ones available as well. For a list of free, high-grade programming books see: GitHub.com/vhf/free-programming-books. Once you have a pretty good grasp of the theory, and you've moved onto writing code, I recommend bookmarking StackOverflow.com as a good launchpad for any further issues you may encounter during development.

Over the next four steps, we will be covering some language-independent good practices you can follow when developing each feature of your software. The advice I give in this chapter should be applicable to almost anything you write, but considering how many variations in programming semantics and paradigms there are, I may unintentionally enter into some grey areas. At the very least, even if a suggestion I make can't be applied directly to your project, it should be indirectly applicable to some degree.

Step 2: Lay a solid foundation

Before you can add any code to your project, you first

need a project to which you can add it. Start by creating a minimal project structure that is empty yet complete. By this I mean that even though the project may have no useful code in it, depending on the language, it should at least compile or run reliably. Try to reduce this act of "building" your project down to one, easy-to-perform action, and consider adding a short "INSTALL" file describing the process to other developers. At this early stage, if applicable to your software, it may also be worth putting the necessary pieces into place for cross platform support as well, since adding this later can become increasingly difficult. Getting your project to this state will allow you to make your first commit to version control, and will give you a solid foundation on which to start building.

Another feature you should enable or add to your project is some form of automated code validation. This can either be a separate tool that you run against your project, or built into the compilation of your source code. Either way, try to incorporate running these checks as part of the "build" action you configured above. This will allow you to fix each mistake as soon as it is introduced, rather than letting them pile up and become unmanageable later.

Whether you're using compiler warnings or an external application, be sure to set the warning level of your chosen tool as high as you can possibly tolerate, and prefer to resolve issues by fixing code rather than reducing the level. While code validation can be very helpful in preventing potential bugs, be careful that you do not become too dependant on it.

Every feature and bug fix you do should be traceable back to a particular release of your software. One way to effectively manage this via VCS is to branch from trunk for each version number. Each of these branches can then act as a staging area for all changes made between releases. In other words, initially you could create a branch series named: "0.1", then for every feature or bug fix you tackle, you could branch off further from that series, merging back to "0.1" as each task is completed. Alternatively, you could create a branch from trunk named: "devel" to which all project development is committed, then create snapshots of this branch for: "0.1", "0.2", etc. when needed. The latter is my personal preference as it allows for picking a version number upon release, rather than having to specify it up front. Once you are happy with the changes staged in an "x.y" branch, merging it back to trunk marks the official release of that version. Branching this way creates a really clean, easy-to-navigate commit history, allowing you to retrieve detailed change logs of every version of your software, and recall exactly when and where each feature and bug fix was released.

There are two important rules to follow when using version control: commit everything, and commit often. What you commit to your VCS should be anything (other than build artifacts of course) that undergoes change during the development of your software. That means: your project structure should not only comprise of code, it should incorporate its documentation as well, including any notes and to-do lists you feel are worth versioning. This leaves you with an incredibly useful, combined history of all changes, for all elements of your product, and eliminates the redundancy of having to maintain each aspect of your project separately. Committing changes often is a good habit to have for many more reasons, namely: it encourages a steady flow of updates into the project, resulting in small, easy-to-read diffs, it allows you and others to easily pick up from where you last left off, your latest work is always kept backed up safely on a secure remote server, and as long as you ensure that no commit breaks the "build", it gives you the fine-grained ability to rollback changes one-by-one if needed.

Step 3: Design a user-friendly user interface

Jef Raskin, the man who conceived and initiated the Apple Mac project, put it best when he said: "As far as the customer is concerned, the interface is the product". As we discussed in chapter 3, whether or not your software will have a User Interface, it should at least have an Application Programming Interface. An API essentially comprises of a collection of types and functions made available to developers, including yourself, for creating applications. While an API is the interface to your back-end, a UI is the interface to your API, hence, any good UI design begins with the design of a good API. A good API should be easy to use correctly, and difficult to use incorrectly. To ensure this, prefer simple over complex always, use standard types in your function signatures as much as possible, and avoid long parameter lists.

While every API is fundamentally made up of types and functions, depending on the programming language and paradigm used, they can be grouped or further broken down into a hierarchy of entities such as: frameworks, modules, libraries, namespaces, classes, prototypes, and structures. Regardless of how you choose to assemble your project's architecture, your focus should be on designing 20% of the entities that define 80% of your API's functionality. Furthermore, every entity in your API should have only one well-defined, cohesive responsibility. Prefer creating small entities that closely model the problem domain, over large ones that are abstract in purpose. Small entities are easier to write, easier to test, and in the end, easier to use.

Your API should exist to help its users, not to dump complex responsibilities onto them, therefore, try not to return results from functions that implicitly require careful management, such as: expecting users to destroy it in a particular manner, or trusting them not to change its state later. Possibly the worst offence you can commit in this respect, is giving out direct handles to your entities' internals, then expecting the receiver to behave with them. Only make public what should be public, and encapsulate the rest. You can hide an API's internals by placing them in files that are physically separate from its headers, or by using language features to logically restrict their visibility via the public interface. This gives you, as the API developer, fine-grained access control over the private entities of your project, resulting in a safer, more reliable product for your users.

Forming relationships between the entities of an API is both natural and dangerous at the same time. Strongly coupled code is very difficult to maintain, and near impossible to reuse. Any change made to one entity not only requires a deep understanding of every other entity it's connected to, it often requires that changes be made to all of them collectively in order to keep the combined logic synchronised. One way of avoiding strong coupling in your code, is to prefer dependency injection over inheritance wherever possible. This means giving an entity its dependencies by means of input parameters to its construction, rather than creating one complex entity with all behaviours combined.

A major exception to the above rule is inheriting from abstract interfaces. An abstract interface is an entity specifically designed to be inherited. It has no behaviour, just a set of function declarations that its child entities must implement. I say this is an exception because, as the name suggests, this type of entity should actually make up most of your public interface. These interfaces are also instrumental in abstracting away third-party APIs, avoiding tight coupling between your code and its dependencies. Together with abstract interfaces, consider building an entity that provides a means for creating objects without having to specify their child types (A.K.A. an "Abstract Factory"). To further combat coupling between entities, avoid sharing any global data between them, and where stronger relationships are required, dependency inject the entities into another whose own cohesive purpose is to manage them.

As you construct your API feature-by-feature, add placeholder comments to each new entity you define, formatted accordingly for your document generator to pick up. You may want to insert a few brief descriptions into these comments as you add them, but these may change as you implement the back-end, so leaving them blank is good enough for now. Remember also to prepend the appropriate notices to the top of every new source file you create, in accordance with your project's license terms. Details on how to specifically apply a license to your work can be found at: OpenSource.org/licenses.

Step 4: Put your interface to the test

For every bug and wish list item you tackle, you should ensure at least two things: that the new code you add works correctly, and that by adding it, you do not break any existing code. This can be achieved by writing a set of test applications that, when run, will execute a sequence of queries against your API, and verify that the resulting behaviour exhibited is as expected. Retrofitting tests to a project becomes increasingly difficult, sometimes even impossible, the longer it is put off. For that reason, writing these test applications should really form part of the development process itself. Of course, there are other reasons why tests should be written together with the features they probe: it forces you to see your user interface from the user's point of view, it gives developers a good feel of how the API is used, and while new tests verify that new functionality works, existing tests ensure that existing functionality is not broken by it.

There are two main types of testing: unit and integration. Unit (or "white box") testing verifies the behaviour of a software entity in isolation, while integration (or "black box") testing verifies the behaviour of multiple entities interacting with each other. During unit testing, to ensure that an entity is properly isolated, its dependencies must be replaced by "mock" entities that exhibit well-defined test behaviour. This requirement is yet another circumstance where abstract interfaces and dependency injection become indispensable to your API. In fact, considering that tests are written solely against interfaces, your API is really all that is needed to begin writing them, and is precisely why this step immediately follows its design. Later, as you implement your back-end, private interfaces may start to form as well. In terms of unit testing, these interfaces should be treated the same way.

By now we have established that each feature you add to your software should begin with applying the appropriate API updates, followed immediately by writing tests for them. A similar attitude should be applied to bug fixes. When fixing a bug in your code, the first thing you should do is write a "regression test" that exposes the issue. This test should simulate the conditions of the bug such that it is designed to fail. With this failing test in place, you can proceed with fixing the bug until it passes reliably. Don't let yourself be discouraged by how long you spend developing test code. It is perfectly acceptable for one to spend more time writing code that verifies new logic, than it takes to implement the logic itself. As Albert Einstein put it: "If I had an hour to solve a problem, I'd spend 55 minutes thinking about the problem, and 5 minutes thinking about solutions".

Tests should be written to enforce reliability. Reliable software not only means that it should work when expected to work, it also means failing safely when things go wrong. Unfortunately, it is very common for people to write tests that focus purely on the former, and overlook the latter. Well-defined error conditions are just as much a part of your product's intended functionality as its non-error conditions are, therefore, each should be tested as thoroughly as the other. You might want to invest some time into finding a good "test coverage" tool for your project as well. These tools are useful in pointing out what logic in your code is not "covered" by your tests, and hence, can help you achieve a better overall "test coverage".

Once you have assembled some form of test suite, try to

incorporate running it as part of the unified "build" action you configured in step 2. An automated test suite will allow you to ensure that, when making any changes to your code, the product remains in working order. This gives users a reason to trust in your software, and ease of mind even when major refactoring is required.

Step 5: Implement to the interface design

At this stage of the development cycle, you should have an interface to your new feature declared, and a few tests in place to verify its proposed behaviour. Now it's time to implement that behaviour, and consequently, get your tests to pass. It's important to bare in mind here, that although "what" your feature does may pass your tests, there are a lot of mistakes still to be made in "how" it is implemented. Poorly written software is a maintenance nightmare for everybody involved, and more often than not, ends up being abandoned entirely. For each feature you implement, again, prefer simple over complex, correct over fast, and safe over insecure. When writing functions: prefer short over long, and flat over nested. A complex function is a good indication that its entity does not have a single, cohesive responsibility, and therefore, should be broken down further into smaller parts.

As we have learnt, part of ensuring the reliability of our software, is to fail safely when things go wrong. To this end, you should establish a rational error handling policy for your project, and stick to it consistently throughout the code. Regardless of which policy you apply, errors should be emitted in a way that is as easy to catch, as they are easy to understand. An error should aim to provide enough diagnostic detail to the user such that it is explicitly clear as to what went wrong, and hence, can assist in resolving the issue, either by them directly, or by you via bug report. Some details that are particularly useful in an error message are: a timestamp, an error type, its severity level, a detailed description of the error condition, and the position in code where the fault occurred (In fact, this sort of detail is useful in just about any log message your project emits). It is also crucial that you do not penalise your users unnecessarily for low severity issues. Know when a function should rollback its changes and error out completely, and when it should simply emit a warning and continue.

When designing your interface, I mentioned that globally

shared data between entities should be avoided wherever possible. Clearly the same attitude should be carried over to your implementation. Shared data not only increases coupling, it causes contention, which needlessly reduces performance, but more importantly, can become extremely difficult to maintain. Try to declare variables as locally to where they are needed as possible. The shorter their lifetimes, the less state you will have to maintain. Although this approach may cause duplication of data, sometimes redundancy can be justified in order to reduce coupling. One exception to this rule is the use of globally shared constants. Contrary to what some people may believe, programming is not magic, so do try to avoid using magic numbers. Rather declare all required constants in some common area of your project where they are easy to find and adjust, than have them scattered amongst your code as raw values. Lastly, avoid cyclic dependencies between entities as well. Only call functions that are immediately related to the entity in which they are called, and where entities need to interact, inject them into a manager in which they can be observed.

As you introduce each feature to your software, you should add documentation for all public entities of the

API, and comments to all private elements of the code. For each entity you implement, update your API documentation by filling in the placeholders you added in step 3. These notes should clearly describe how each entity of the API is used, and explain in detail how each will behave under different inputs. Now and then, take a moment to run your document generator and make sure that the output looks correct. Alternatively, you could dynamically generate your documentation as yet another part of the project's "build" action.

Summary

Step 1: Speak your project's language

- Investigating into your chosen programming language should naturally form part of research.

- In software engineering, theory can not be fully appreciated until it is practiced.

- I'd recommend that you start with a good book or two on the subject.

- For free and non-free books see: GitHub.com/vhf/free-programming-books and Amazon.com.

Step 2: Lay a solid foundation

- Start with a minimum project structure that "builds" with one, easy-to-perform action.
- Add automatic code validation as part of your project's "build".
- Branch from trunk for each version such that all changes can be traced back to a release.
- When it comes to using version control: commit everything, and commit often.

Step 3: Design a user-friendly user interface

- Any good UI design begins with the design of a good API.
- Prefer simple over complex, use standard types, and avoid long parameter lists.
- Every entity in your API should have only one well-defined, cohesive responsibility.
- Your API should exist to help its users, not to dump complex responsibilities onto them.
- Strongly coupled code is very difficult to maintain, and near impossible to reuse.
- Prefer dependency injection over inheritance, with the exception of abstract interfaces.
- Add document generator placeholders to each

new entity you define.

Step 4: Put your interface to the test

- Write a set of applications that, when run, will execute a sequence of tests against your API.
- New tests verify that new code works, and existing tests ensure that existing code still works.
- There are two main types of testing: unit (or "white box") and integration (or "black box").
- When fixing a bug in your code, the first thing you should do is write a "regression test".
- Your error conditions should be tested as thoroughly as your non-error conditions.
- Incorporate running tests as part of your project's "build".

Step 5: Implement to the interface design

- Prefer simple over complex, correct over fast, and safe over insecure.
- Establish a rational error handling policy for your project, and stick to it consistently.
- Avoid sharing global data between entities.
- Update your API documentation by filling in the placeholders you added in step 3.

PART FOUR

Deliver

CHAPTER EIGHT
Releasing your project

Step 1: Pick a version numbering scheme

Before we move on to preparing our software for its initial release, we must first decide on how it will be versioned. Whether or not your project includes a UI, it should be primarily versioned in relation to the state of its API. A version number not only allows people to gauge roughly how much older their copy of the API is relative to current, it gives users an indication of the level of compatibility one release has with another. In order to satisfy these conditions, you should establish a version numbering scheme up front, then stick to it consistently throughout the lifetime of your project. Providing a reliable versioning policy for your software naturally promotes confidence in the reliability of the product itself.

The most commonly used versioning scheme amongst both open and closed source projects, is the three-component numbering system. In a typical three-component system, the first component is the major number, the second is the minor, and the third is the micro (E.g. "2.4.0"). Changes to the micro number within the same major and minor version should be both forward- and backward-compatible, changes to the minor number within the same major version should be at least backward-compatible, and changes to the major number can be both forward- and backward-incompatible. Considering that this policy is so widely used and recognised, it is a good idea to apply it to your projects. However, it is not uncommon for some software to exclude the micro number entirely and use a simpler two-component system. Both are good choices, but again, try to pick just one and stick with it.

Another component that can be useful as a postfix to your software's version number, is its current development status. By being open and honest about the stability of your product, your users will know what to expect, and may even be more impressed if it turns out to be more stable than anticipated. There are a number of ways to describe the stability of a release, but the most commonly accepted are: "alpha" (E.g. "1.0-alpha"), "beta" (E.g. "1.0-beta"), and "stable" (E.g. "1.0"). "Alpha" signifies an early edition of your software that contains all functionality intended for the release, but is also known to contain some notable bugs, while "beta" indicates that although bugs may still be present, all serious issues have been resolved. Leading up to version 1.0 however, you could indicate to users that your software is still in early development by publishing a series of iterations under major version 0 (E.g. 0.1, 0.2, etc.), until it is functionally complete enough for its first significant release.

Earlier I mentioned two directions to software compatibility: forward and backward. Forward-compatibility means that code using version X of your API can be downgraded to X-1 without change, and backward-compatibility means that code using version X of your API can be upgraded to X+1 without change. Of course, the definition of "change" also depends on the type of compatibility enforced.

There are three major types of software compatibility: binary, source, and functional. Binary compatibility means that an application using version X of your API can be upgraded to X+1 without having to rebuild the application, while source compatibility means that an application using version X of your API can be upgraded to X+1 without having to change the source code. If your project produces a library in binary form, breaking binary compatibility is both forward- and backward-incompatible, therefore effects the major version of your software. In order for your users to easily gauge whether a new version of your library will be binary compatible with an existing application, include the major and minor version numbers as a postfix to its name (E.g. "MyLibrary2.4"). Lastly, functional compatibility means that code using version X of your API can be upgraded to X+1 without any behavioural consequences.

Step 2: Clean up your project structure

As soon as you've implemented the minimum number of wish list items required for your project to become usable, put all development on hold a moment, isolate a snapshot of the code into its own dedicated staging branch, and shift into release mode. The first step you need to take towards preparing your project for release, is to clean up its file structure. Depending on the current state of your project, this can entail rearranging its directories to match a certain layout your users may expect to see, or adding a few files that are commonly found in other open source projects.

Regardless of whether you agree with the saying: "a cluttered desk is a sign of a cluttered mind", it certainly appears that way when seen from an outsider's point of view. A similar impression is made on visitors when they see how your project is laid out. Unfortunately, a messy file structure strongly implies that the contents of those files are messy as well. Conversely, if I see a project's externals arranged cleanly, I immediately assume that its internals received the same care. A project structure that is recognisable, or at least easy to navigate, will allow your users to quickly adapt to it, as opposed to losing interest if it takes too long to understand.

Ultimately, you should aim to arrange your directory structure according to the conventions found in projects similar to yours, and because it is typically the programming language that determines which conventions are followed, this can be pretty easy to discern. Simply search for a few popular open source projects written in the language you're using, identify any obvious patterns in file structure amongst them, and try not to deviate too far from these unless you absolutely must. Although it should not be necessary, you may also want to spend a little more time comparing projects that are both in and out of your specific problem domain, in case any additional standards apply. As I've already revealed, my default for finding open source software is SourceForge.net, but considering that we're particularly interested in seeing how projects arrange their files, GitHub.com is my site of choice here.

Irrespective of what folders make up your project's directory structure, users may expect to find at least one or two standard files in its root, the most common being: "CHANGES", "COPYING" or "LICENSE", "INSTALL", and "README". We will get into the finer details of what goes into each of these in the next step, but for now, you can just create them and leave them blank.

Step 3: Update internal documentation

Releasing an open source project, as the name suggests, invites developers to download and build the source themselves. By extending such an invitation, it is vitally important that the process of building and utilising your code is as clear and straightforward as possible. To achieve this, your project should provide some high-level developer documentation that is as easy to find, as it is easy to follow.

Open source software that is difficult to build is practically useless to developers. The situation typically plays out like this: a developer visits an open source project website, out of interest they download the source code, after 10 minutes of failing to build it, they give up, remove the software, and look for another alternative. To clarify, I'm not suggesting that if a build takes longer than 10 minutes to execute, your visitors will give up on it. Obviously there is a difference between wasting time getting nowhere, and spending time getting somewhere.

Taking the above into consideration, possibly the most important internal document your project could include is an "INSTALL" file. This file should contain some easy-to-follow guidelines on how to build and install your software. When it comes to building, more effort should always equal more reward. For example, if your build procedure is unavoidably complex, or differs significantly from platform to platform, consider abstracting these difficulties behind a script that can be run as a single action. Again, do try to include running tests as part of this process. This way, developers can confidently gauge whether or not their build completed successfully.

Once downloaded, the first document any user is likely to open is your "README" file. This should be a plain text document stating the current release version, followed by a brief description of what your software does. Seeing that this file will be the starting block for most people, it should also provide some references to other useful resources such as: the project website, and the "INSTALL" file where developers can find build instructions. Of course, as I've seen in many projects, you may prefer to omit the "INSTALL" file completely by simply appending your build instructions to the end of the "README" file.

Another document that is important to both users and

developers is the "COPYING" or "LICENSE" file. This should contain the full license text for the license your project is being released under. Not only is this required for legal purposes, it allows others to easily identify your software's terms of distribution, as well as to determine if and how your code can be integrated into theirs. Full license texts for all popular open source licenses can be found at: OpenSource.org/licenses.

Last but not least, consider including a "CHANGES" file in your project's root as well. At the top of this file should be a heading stating the current version of your software, under which the key changes made in this release can be listed. This list does not need to be as extensive as your project's change log, but should state just the most important high-level improvements introduced into the latest version. As you release each iteration of your software, prepend the new list of changes to this file such that each set of release notes appears in reverse chronological order from top to bottom.

Step 4: Update external documentation

As an open source software developer, you will have at

least 2 clients: other developers, and potential employers. If your software is a full-blown application, you will have a 3rd: end-users. The difference between end-users and developers, is that the former will unlikely ever see your project's internals, and hence, will learn about your software purely by what is presented on its website. Considering that your potential employers may or may not be developers themselves, your project's external documentation should always be designed such that it alone can make a good impression on its readers.

Regardless of whether a client is a developer or an end-user however, at least the first thing they will learn about your project is what its website looks like. As we touched on earlier, a newcomer whose first impression of your software is bad, will seldom give it a second chance later. That in mind, it's not a good idea to cut corners on your project's outward appearance. In fact, if you only had time to properly prepare one form of documentation, without a doubt, you should prioritise external over internal.

During development, you added specially formatted comments to your code in order for your document generator to collect and output API documentation. While this means a lot of the hard work for your website is done, you will still need to provide some sort of surfacing material. Most document generators support adding custom pages to their output, so creating a homepage should really be as easy as adding another formatted comment. At the very least, this page should contain an introduction briefly describing what your software does, and one or two tutorials demonstrating how the API is used. Other useful information could include: a features list, a requirements list, a short "getting started" guide to downloading and navigating the project directory, example outputs or screenshots, and release notes taken directly from your "CHANGES" file.

The home page described above is clearly targeted at developers, if your software is also an application, you will want to create a separate home for your end-users as well. This should then be made the primary landing page for your website, with a link or tab to the developer section for those interested in getting the source. What goes onto this page should roughly follow the same format as its developer variant, but described instead from the end-user's perspective.

Finally, don't forget to update your canned hosting project page with any new information that may have been changed or introduced since it was last edited. Further resources to consider providing at a later stage could be: a thorough project design document, and a complete end-user manual.

Step 5: Package and release

Throughout this chapter so far, we have been running through what is known as "release stabilisation". This is the process whereby a snapshot of your software is isolated and conditioned into a releasable state. As we have seen, at a minimum this can entail: picking a version number, cleaning up your file structure, and updating documentation. Stabilisation may also entail: deciding which changes should be included in the current release, and filtering out those that should be deferred to the next. As soon as your staging branch is stabilised and ready to launch, it's time to package it up and make it available for download.

Although it may not be that difficult for users to obtain a

copy of your software directly from VCS, even the simplest of version control systems will require at least twice as much effort than clicking a link. Providing an easy way to get ahold of your releases will not only keep your current users happy, it will open up your software to a lot more visitors that may simply want to download it out of curiosity. If your project is also an end-user application, you especially cannot expect them to get a copy from VCS. In fact, in this case, you will need to provide two separate downloads: one for an archive of the source, and another for an archive of the resultant application, built and ready to use.

Observe the following steps when releasing a new version of your software: merge your staging branch into trunk with a commit message consisting of release notes from the "CHANGES" file, merge trunk back into your other development branches to synchronise them with any stabilisation updates, package your project directory into an archive labeled: the product name plus version number postfix (E.g. "MyLibrary-2.4.0.zip"), and if your project results in either an application or binary of any form, consider building it for each supported platform, then packaging each into an archive labeled: the product name plus version number and platform postfix (E.g. "MyLibrary-2.4.0-Linux_x86-64.zip").

Once you have packaged your software, you'll need to find somewhere online to put it. As far as I've seen, all canned hosting sites provide some form of file hosting. This is probably the simplest and most effective option you have. Not only does this mean your releases can be maintained in the same place as the source, they will be centrally available for download, making them both easy to find, and easy to get. Simply upload your archives to the "Downloads" or "Releases" page of your project, and you're done!

Summary

Step 1: Pick a version numbering scheme

- Pick a numbering scheme up front then version your software in relation to the state of its API.
- The most common versioning scheme is the three-component system. (E.g. "2.4.0")
- Sometimes development status can be useful as a postfix to your version (E.g. "2.4.0-alpha")
- There are two directions to software

compatibility: forward and backward.

- There are three major types of software compatibility: binary, source, and functional.

Step 2: Clean up your project structure

- Isolate a snapshot of your project into a staging branch and start cleaning up its file structure.
- A messy file structure strongly implies that the contents of those files are messy as well.
- Follow conventions used in other popular open source projects by browsing GitHub.com.
- Create files for: "CHANGES", "COPYING" / "LICENSE", "INSTALL", and "README".

Step 3: Update internal documentation

- Building and utilising your code should be made as clear and straightforward as possible.
- "INSTALL" should contain simple guidelines on how to build and install your software.
- "README" should contain the version, a brief description, and links to other resources.
- "COPYING" or "LICENSE" should contain the full license text for your project's license.
- "CHANGES" should contain high-level release

notes in reverse chronological order.

Step 4: Update external documentation

- External documentation should be designed such that it alone can make a good impression.
- First impressions last, so don't cut corners on your project's outward appearance.
- Use your documentation generator to create a home page for your website.
- If your software is an application, create separate home pages for developers and end-users.
- Keep your canned hosting project page updated.

Step 5: Package and release

- Provide an easy way to download your source code as an archive.
- If your software results in an application or binary, provide separate archives per platform.
- Stabilise your release, merge it to trunk, re-sync development branches, then package.
- Upload your archives to the "Downloads" section of your canned hosting project page.

CHAPTER NINE

Marketing and maintaining your software

Step 1: Raise awareness of your project

You've done it! You've released your very own open source project! Now it's time to start acquiring users. The earlier you can get people using and thinking about your software, the earlier you will get feedback on whether it is as appealing as you hoped it would be. Early feedback can allow you to make critical decisions about the direction in which to take your project before it has gained too much momentum for it to pivot any further.

Your first target audience should be early adopters. An early adopter is a person who will start using a product or technology as soon as it becomes available, and hence is usually the sort of user who will be alright with hitting a few bugs here and there. You won't have to look very far to find worthy candidates for this audience. In fact, the best people to invite as early adopters to your software are the ones around you. Simply ask your friends and work colleagues to download the project and give it a try, but only provide them with a link to its home page. This way they will get a taste of the entire end-to-end experience of learning about it, acquiring it, and running it themselves. Presuming they are capable of being somewhat impartial, the great thing about having people you know test out your software, is that it can be far easier to take their initial criticisms than that of complete strangers.

From the crowd of adopters above, try to narrow down one or two people you personally trust to give you a more in-depth review of the code as well. Eventually you'll want to begin requesting formal reviews of your branches from other developers online, but for now this is a really nice informal way to ease into the review process. Don't be discouraged if you battle to find anyone you know who is willing to do this, give it some time, your software will inevitably reach these kinds of people anyway. As soon as your project has gained enough interest such that you are able to request reviews from remote developers, your users' confidence in your work will easily double knowing that multiple engineers have seen and approved of it.

By identifying people skilled enough to review your code, you may have simultaneously identified some potential contributors. Once your early adopters have been given enough time to try out and review the product, why not extend an invitation to them for their contribution to it. Again, don't be disappointed if nobody around you is interested or has the time to help, at this point it's just worth asking.

One last group of early adopters you should reach out to, are those who are already visiting your project page. Without having done any real marketing of your own, these visitors are finding your software not only because they are searching specifically for what it offers, but because they're choosing it from their list of possible options. Essentially, these are the clients who are finding you, rather than you having to find them. For this group of people, each time you launch a new release worthy of note, place an announcement at the top of your project page or website inviting them to download it. You may also want to briefly describe the product's most significant updates as part of the announcement to further invoke their interest.

Step 2: Market yourself

Prior to marketing your project, you should bare in mind that your software is not the only thing going public here. As an open source developer, people are watching you almost as much as they're watching your work, so it is vitally important that you present the former with as much care as you do the latter. An inspiring quote that springs to mind here is that of Arthur Rock. As Silicon Valley venture capitalist and early investor in Apple Computer and Intel, Arthur Rock once stated: "What I'm interested in is investing in people".

The first step to making yourself as approachable as your software, is to open up some public channels of communication. This could simply mean providing an email address on your project's home page with a friendly message encouraging people to contact you, but could extend to starting a dedicated discussion forum, or perhaps an instant messaging channel via services such as:

IRC, Slack, or Jabber. Regardless of whether anyone will ever require the support, people are more likely to use your software knowing that you're willing to provide it. Of course, it's completely up to you which contact details you wish to make public.

Just as you have been open and honest about the capabilities of your software, you should be open and honest in absolutely everything you say about it. Irrespective of whether you're speaking via public or private channels, never assume that a lie will go unnoticed. After all, the truth is in the source, and the source is wide open.

Equally important as being honest, is being polite. Avoid being rude to anyone, even toward those who come across as rude to you. This includes bashing your competition. By no means should you ever take a stab at another project in the hope that it will increase your credibility. Nine times out of ten a remark like this will only leave you looking belligerent and insecure. In all situations, try to see your words as others see them. Kindness can be contagious, even to the hardest of hearts.

Overall, keep in mind that for most people using your software, the only version of you they will ever come to know, is the one you present through written word. You may be an extremely intelligent and focused person, but if your correspondence with people is unorganised, incomplete, or hard to follow, they will believe that to be who you are. Again, empathise with your audience, see yourself as they may see you, and present yourself as professionally as you wish to be treated.

Step 3: Market your project

Now that you have tested the waters a bit with some early adopters, and perhaps made a few adjustments in response to their feedback, you should be ready to take your software to market. In this step I want to share with you three really simple direct and indirect marketing strategies I have found to work well. The idea here is not to force your product down people's throats like a bad advertising campaign. We simply want to put your software in the right places such that people who are actually looking for it will find it.

Let's begin with a very easy indirect marketing strategy:

making your software more widely available. To achieve this you will want to get your project onto a couple of free download sites. As you can imagine, there are a ton of these out there, fortunately however, it only takes one of them to pick up your software for the others to start hosting it too. From experience, I can recommend that you begin by posting your project on Softpedia.com. This service is both clean and very popular, so through it, you will inevitably reach a lot of people, and by people I also mean other websites. Once your software picks up a bit of momentum here, you will start to see it popping up all over the web. Adding a project to Softpedia.com is fairly straightforward: just browse to their home page, find the "Submit Applications" link, and fill in the form. This is where it gets even better: To the best of their ability, the guys at Softpedia will actually take care of ensuring that your software is kept up-to-date on their site, so you won't have to! If you do want to personally submit an update, all you have to do is send them an email, and they'll sort out the rest. Follow the "Send us updates" link on their home page to find the appropriate contact details.

The second marketing strategy is more focused on directly targeting those who are looking for a product like yours, but are struggling to find it. In this approach, you will want to search the web for questions that your software solves, and propose your solution as an answer to them. When it comes to developer Q&A, there is really only one site worth mentioning here: StackOverflow.com. Browse to StackOverflow.com, search for a few keywords that describe your software, then try to identify any problems that could be solved by using it. When answering these questions, do make sure to explicitly state that the product you're punting is your own. Not only is it good etiquette to do this, you will likely be banned from the site if you do not. Remember, you're being watched.

Another form of the above method of marketing is contributing to online forums. For this, Groups.Google.com is a great place to start. On Google Groups you can either search for an existing forum on which to post your solution, or create an entirely new discussion under a group that you feel may find your work interesting. Either way, try not to spam loosely related forums with your software as an effort to extend its reach. This will likely do more harm to your reputation than good.

Step 4: Keep an eye out for bugs and questions

At this stage of your project's life, progress will begin to take on two forms: new feature development, and current feature maintenance. As your software acquires users, you can expect bug reports to start trickling in at any point. Unfortunately, it can be easy to forget about the maintenance side of development when engrossed in the thrill of writing new features. While adding functionality to your software is a good idea, turning your back on users in order to do it is not.

Make an effort to check on your project's bug tracker at least once a week. Most people will be alright with waiting a few days to get a reply, but anything longer than a week or two may give them the impression that your project is inactive. One way to ensure that you keep an eye on your bugs is to regularly use the tracker yourself. In the same way that you added wish list items to the bug tracker when creating and configuring your project, you should also add any bugs you uncover during its development. This way, others that run into these issues will see that they are known, and can feel more at ease knowing that solutions to them have been scheduled. One very important matter to note here is that there is a difference between handling regular bugs, and dealing with security vulnerabilities. If an issue is brought to your attention that puts users in danger of a serious security breach, immediately remove any trace of the issue from all public channels, and deal with the problem privately until a fix is available.

Some canned hosting sites will allow you to provide a separate area for Q&A. If you have something like this set up, as often as you check on your bugs, you should check on your questions. Submitting your own questions is yet another great way to keep tabs on what your users are saying, as well as an effective means of providing some FAQs for them to learn from. As in the previous step, now and then, check StackOverflow.com again for any new questions related to your software. You may even start to find specific enquiries about your project showing up as more people discover it.

When replying to bug reports and feature requests, be friendly, but don't be a pushover. Stay true to your product "not" list. If somebody requests an update that goes beyond the scope of your product, politely inform them that the feature unfortunately does not fit within the project plans, then add the item to your bug tracker with the status: "invalid", "won't fix" or similar. I have personally experienced situations where others have forked a project of mine because I was not willing to add a feature they wanted. If this happens to you, don't be discouraged. By forking, they're really just relieving you of the problem. Consider the issue resolved and continue working on your software as normal. Besides, provided your project is kept maintained, it's relatively uncommon for people to prefer a knockoff over the original anyway.

Step 5: Establish a rational update policy

There is a well-known saying by Leonardo da Vinci that goes: "Art is never finished, only abandoned". Much the same can be said about software. Very rarely is a project "done". The systems we create form part of a much larger computing ecosystem that is constantly evolving around them. Those that can't adapt and improve at a comparative rate will eventually fall behind, and in a lot of cases, are made obsolete by other more up-to-date alternatives. Of course, that's not to say that abandoning a project is necessarily a bad thing. Sometimes it can be a really smart idea to drop one direction and take another. A brilliant manager of mine, Thomas Strehl once said: "The way I distinguish a good engineer from a great one, is how willing they are to throw away their hard work for a better solution".

While maintenance of your software includes keeping it regularly updated, releasing too often can actually irritate your users more than excite them. Retrieving and applying an update is not always a trivial task. Putting your users in a position where they're having to do this more than once or twice a month can become extremely expensive, especially to those using your software in a commercial environment. If the cost of keeping up with your software is higher than the value it offers, people will be forced to find an alternative that is less volatile. With the exception of major bug fixes such as obvious crashes or security vulnerabilities, try to pool your changes into updates you can roll out every two weeks or so.

When updating your software, remember to keep your documentation up-to-date as well, although, bare in mind that it can also be updated independent of any changes to the code. If your users are asking a lot of questions, or reporting bugs that turn out to be misunderstandings, it can be a good sign that your documentation needs work. Don't postpone this kind of update to the next release though. Simply branch from trunk, amend, merge, and re-sync your development branches.

Once you've gotten your software to a point where it is reasonably stable, and you feel you've learnt enough from it, put it aside and move on to the next. As you start to accumulate projects however, it can become a little harder to determine when each should be updated again. One way of handling this is to first establish how popular they are, then apply updates to them only when that demand drops. Most canned hosting sites that provide file hosting will provide some form of download statistics as well. Assuming that your project is somewhat successful, you can roughly measure its popularity by how frequently it's acquired. A noticeable decrease in your project's download rate will usually mean that your regular visitors already have the latest version, and that new visitors are choosing not to download it. There can be many reasons why people would choose not to download your software: there could be a newer, better alternative available, your last update could've happened too long ago, or perhaps the decline in popularity itself is causing others to lose interest. Either way, at this point it's clear that your project is becoming less popular, and hence, could probably do with a little freshening up.

Summary

Step 1: Raise awareness of your project

- The earlier you can get people using your software, the earlier you will get feedback.
- Ask friends and colleagues to be early adopters to your software.
- Find one or two of the above to give you a more in-depth review of the code as well.
- Extend an invitation to your reviewers to contribute to the project.
- Announce each noteworthy release at the top of your project page or website.

Step 2: Market yourself

- Bare in mind that you are being watched almost as much as your work.
- Open up some public channels of communication.

- Be open and honest in everything you say about your software.
- Avoid being rude to anyone, even towards those who come across as rude to you.
- Present yourself as professionally as you would like to be treated.

Step 3: Market your project

- Don't force your project down people's throats like a bad advertising campaign.
- Post your project on Softpedia.com so that it can be picked up by other download sites.
- Provide your software as a solution to any related questions on StackOverflow.com.
- Contribute to forums on Groups.Google.com where people may be interested in your work.

Step 4: Keep an eye out for bugs and questions

- Don't forget about the maintenance side of software development.
- Log your own bugs to keep tabs on the others, and deal with security issues discretely.
- Check StackOverflow.com and your own Q&A services as often as you do your bug tracker.

- Don't be a pushover, stay true to your product "not" list.

Step 5: Establish a rational update policy

- Software is never finished, only abandoned, but that's not necessarily a bad thing.
- Don't release too frequently, it can irritate your users and become extremely expensive.
- Keep your documentation up-to-date, even between releases.
- Once a project is stable, move on to the next, and update it again only when popularity drops.

EPILOGUE

I'd like to take this opportunity to say thank you for reading this book, and if you have managed to release a project along the way, seriously, congratulations! You're one step closer to landing the job you've always wanted, and that is no small achievement by any means! Go ahead and add that to your résumé! The experience you've gained here, and can now irrefutably demonstrate through your hard work, will certainly earn you the respect you deserve, not only from future employers, but from the open source community as well.

So, what should you do once you've released your first project? Write some more! Turn back to the technologies and domains you assembled in Part 1, and continue down the list project-by-project until you feel you've gained enough experience to take on that dream job. For every project you tackle, refer to Parts 2, 3 and 4 for a quick refresher on each phase of the development process. As soon as you've reached the end of your requirements list, don't hesitate, apply for the job! The great thing about having actually practiced every skill required for the position you're aiming for, is that the interview process can become far easier to face now that you have an intimate understanding of the work involved.

Before I close off, I'd like to stress once more that there should be little to no difference in standard between the software you write for your open source projects, and the work you produce in your day job. While the primary aim of this book has been to provide some guidelines to writing quality open source software, virtually all of the advice contained here can also be applied to the software you develop professionally. Remember, the quality of work your employers see in your open source projects is precisely the kind of work they will expect you to produce on the job, especially if it has anything to do with why they hired you.

Again, thank you for reading this book. I hope you've enjoyed it, and that in the process, you've learnt something new. I wish you all the best for your career! Perhaps our paths will even cross somewhere down the line. Until then, if you have any questions or thoughts about the book, feel free to contact me on: themarcustomlinson@gmail.com.

Good luck!

Made in the USA
Middletown, DE
04 December 2016